The lost last book

Dedication

To the tireless explorers of the cosmos, both real and imagined – the scientists, the dreamers, and the brave souls who dare to gaze into the infinite abyss and seek answers to the universe's most profound mysteries. This book is a testament to your unwavering curiosity and relentless pursuit of knowledge. It is dedicated to those who understand that the greatest adventures lie not just in the far reaches of space, but also in the depths of our own understanding, pushing the boundaries of human knowledge and bravely facing the unknown, even when the stakes are impossibly high and the path ahead is fraught with peril. It's for those who see the beauty in complexity, who find wonder in the seemingly inexplicable, and who believe that even the darkest secrets of the universe can eventually yield to the light of discovery. This is for the relentless, the inquisitive, the courageous—for those who strive to understand not only what is, but also what could be, within the vast and awe-inspiring expanse of the cosmos. To those who dare to dream among the stars, and to those who strive to unravel the threads of reality, revealing its intricate tapestry of existence. This is for you, the intrepid pioneers of knowledge and understanding, the vanguard of a new era of cosmic discovery and exploration. May your spirit of discovery never falter, your curiosity never wanes, and your quest for knowledge forever illuminate the path toward a brighter future.

Preface

The cosmos whispers secrets on the wind of time, a symphony of starlight and gravity, echoing with untold tales of creation and destruction. For centuries, humanity has gazed upon the celestial canvas, yearning to decipher its cryptic messages. "The Lost Last Book" is a journey into that yearning, an exploration of the unknown, interwoven with the fabric of scientific possibility. This book is not merely a work of fiction; it is a testament to our endless fascination with the universe and our persistent desire to understand our place within its grand design. It explores the frontiers of astrophysics, venturing into the realms of dark matter and dark energy, concepts that remain among the most perplexing and captivating enigmas in modern science. But "The Lost Last Book" is more than just a scientific exploration; it is a thrilling narrative, a suspenseful tale of discovery, betrayal, and the ultimate fight for the fate of existence itself. The characters you will encounter are driven by ambition, fear, and a profound sense of responsibility – mirroring our own human struggles and aspirations within the grand scheme of the cosmos. While the science within these pages strives for accuracy, remember that it serves to enhance the narrative, not to define it. The true heart of this story lies in the exploration of human nature within an extraordinary context – a universe that is both breathtakingly beautiful and terrifyingly immense. This preface is not only an introduction but also a promise: prepare to be captivated, challenged, and ultimately, transformed by the wonders and perils revealed within the pages that follow. Prepare to embark on an unforgettable adventure into the deepest mysteries of the universe, and perhaps, into the deepest mysteries of yourself.

Introduction

The universe is a vast and mysterious place, a cosmic ocean teeming with wonders beyond our comprehension. From the birth of stars to the death of galaxies, from the subatomic particles that constitute all of matter to the enigmatic nature of dark matter and dark energy, the cosmos holds secrets that have captivated humanity for millennia. In "The Lost Last Book," we delve into these mysteries, weaving a thrilling narrative around the discovery of an ancient artifact—a book containing knowledge that could rewrite our understanding of existence. This book is not merely a tale of adventure; it is a journey into the heart of science, where the wonders of the cosmos collide with the suspense of a high-stakes thriller. Our protagonist, a brilliant but disgraced astrophysicist named Dr. Aris Thorne, stumbles upon this extraordinary book, unwittingly unleashing a chain of events that will challenge his beliefs, test his courage, and ultimately put the fate of the universe in his hands. He is not alone in this quest. Along his path, he encounters allies and enemies, collaborators and betrayers, all united by a shared fascination with the universe's secrets. Together, they will embark on a perilous odyssey, facing down shadowy organizations, cutting-edge technology, and unexpected twists and turns that will keep you on the edge of your seat. "The Lost Last Book" blends rigorous scientific concepts with a fast-paced, action-packed plot, making it accessible to a wide range of readers. Whether you're a seasoned astrophysicist or simply a curious reader with a thirst for adventure, this book will take you on a journey that will both entertain and enlighten. Prepare to confront the mysteries of dark matter and dark energy, unravel ancient conspiracies, and witness the clash between human ambition and the cosmic forces that shape our reality. Prepare to be swept away by a story that blends the breathtaking beauty of the cosmos with the thrill of a race against time, a story where the fate of the universe hangs in the balance. The journey begins now.

Unearthing the Artifact

The biting Chilean wind whipped around Dr. Aris Thorne, stinging his exposed skin despite the heavy thermal layers beneath his parka. He huddled deeper into the shadow of the ALMA telescope array, the colossal antennas looming like metallic sentinels against the inky canvas of the night sky. The air thinned with altitude, each breath a reminder of his isolation, a fitting backdrop for the momentous discovery he'd just made. It wasn't a new galaxy, a distant quasar, or even a confirmation of dark matter – it was far stranger, far more profound.

He had been meticulously calibrating the Atacama Large Millimeter/submillimeter Array, searching for anomalies in the cosmic microwave background radiation, a faint afterglow of the Big Bang. Instead, he'd found something entirely unexpected – buried beneath a layer of ancient Atacama dust, nestled within a seemingly ordinary rock formation, was a book. Not a book as he'd ever seen one, but an object of impossible material.

It was roughly the size of a standard textbook, bound in a substance that resembled polished obsidian, yet possessed an unnerving weight, a density far beyond any known material. He'd tried to scratch its surface with his multi-tool, expecting to leave a mark, but the obsidian-like surface remained untouched, perfectly smooth and flawlessly black, absorbing light rather than reflecting it. The very air around it seemed to shimmer with an almost imperceptible energy. The "pages," if they could be called that, were not made of paper or parchment, but of some unknown, impossibly thin, yet solid material. Intricate, swirling symbols, unlike any language he had ever encountered, covered every surface.

Thorne felt a surge of adrenaline, a rush of excitement mixed with a chilling apprehension. This wasn't just an archaeological find; this was something... else. He carefully extracted the book, his gloved hands trembling slightly. He knew that this discovery could revolutionize everything, reshape our understanding of the universe, or worse, potentially obliterate it. The weight of responsibility settled heavily on his shoulders, amplifying the already harsh conditions of the high-altitude desert.

The initial scientific analysis, conducted in the cramped confines of his mobile observatory, proved equally baffling. Spectroscopic analysis revealed no known elements in its composition. The book seemingly defied the laws of physics – it lacked any discernible molecular structure, yet it was undeniably solid. Its density suggested a mass far greater than its apparent volume, a physical impossibility according to established scientific principles. The energy signature emanating from the book was faint, but undeniable, oscillating at a frequency outside the known electromagnetic spectrum.

The symbols, alien and complex, were the next puzzle. He'd spent years deciphering ancient Sumerian cuneiform, deciphering Mayan glyphs, and even worked on the Rosetta project attempting to translate unknown extraterrestrial signals. Nothing prepared him for this. The patterns were intricate, mathematically precise, hinting at an advanced understanding of cosmology and astrophysics far beyond human capability. There were recurring motifs – spirals, knotted patterns, and representations that seemed to depict celestial bodies in motion, but in a way that defied conventional gravitational physics.

He knew he couldn't do this alone. The implications were too vast, the potential dangers too significant. The initial secrecy surrounding his discovery was a necessary precaution; he knew that his findings would be met with skepticism, even outright disbelief, from the mainstream scientific community. But worse, he knew that this was not an isolated anomaly; powerful forces, shadows lurking in the dark recesses of global power structures, were already aware of the book's existence.

He'd received an anonymous email shortly after his discovery, a single line of text: "The book is not yours to keep." The sender remained untraceable, but the veiled threat resonated with a chilling clarity. The next email came two days later, this time with an attached file – a satellite image of his observatory, highlighting his location with unnerving

precision. The message was simple: "We are watching."

Thorne's heart pounded in his chest. The weight of his discovery suddenly intensified, not only scientifically, but existentially. He understood, now, that this was no mere academic pursuit; this was a race against time, a high-stakes game of cosmic proportions. This wasn't just about unraveling the book's secrets; it was about protecting them, and perhaps, the universe itself, from a force far more formidable than any he could have ever imagined.

His first steps toward understanding the book involved leveraging every technological resource at his disposal. He accessed the most powerful supercomputers, utilizing advanced AI algorithms designed for pattern recognition and linguistic analysis. The AI devoured the images of the symbols, generating statistical analyses, searching for patterns and potential grammatical structures. The results were, to say the least, unexpected.

The AI identified mathematical relationships within the symbols, suggesting a sophisticated understanding of higher dimensional geometry and complex topological spaces. It flagged recurring patterns related to prime numbers and fractal dimensions, hinting at a civilization with a far deeper grasp of mathematical principles than humankind. The AI even suggested possible links to quantum physics, implying a mastery over manipulating the very fabric of spacetime.

Weeks bled into months, the relentless analysis slowly yielding fragmented translations. Initial attempts yielded snippets of what appeared to be a cosmic history, a chronicle of events far predating humanity. It spoke of a time before the Big Bang, of energies and forces beyond comprehension, of a sentient universe aware of its own existence. There were references to "The Architects," a civilization of unimaginable power and advanced technology, capable of manipulating the very fabric of spacetime. The fragments were tantalizing, but tantalizingly incomplete, akin to reading a single page from a cosmic encyclopedia.

The AI identified several recurring terms – "The Void," "The Weaver," and "The Obsidian Gate" – phrases that suggested a profound understanding of dark matter and dark energy. The descriptions hinted that dark matter was not simply an inert substance, but a conscious entity, a sentient force with its own agenda. The Obsidian Gate, meanwhile, seemed to refer to a gateway or a point of singularity, a pathway to other dimensions or alternate realities.

The implications were staggering. If the book's contents
were true, then everything humanity understood about the
cosmos was fundamentally wrong. The universe wasn't
merely a cold, indifferent expanse of matter and energy,
but a complex, dynamic entity, teeming with unseen forces
and hidden intelligences. The implications for human
existence, for our place in the cosmos, were utterly
transformative.

But the knowledge gained came at a price. The relentless
work fueled paranoia and isolation. Thorne began
experiencing vivid dreams, fragmented visions of swirling
nebulae, monstrous entities, and silent, watchful eyes. The
line between reality and the book's cryptic world started
blurring, leaving him perpetually on edge, haunted by the
whispers of a universe far beyond his understanding. The
weight of his discovery was no longer merely scientific; it
pressed down on him with a crushing psychological
burden. He knew that he needed help, not just in
deciphering the book, but in surviving the consequences of
his discovery. The shadowy organization, "The Obsidian
Order," was not just watching; they were moving. Their
presence became a palpable threat, a chilling reminder of
the stakes involved. His next move had to be strategic,
calculated, and swift. He needed an ally.

Initial Deciphering Attempts

The flickering screen of his laptop cast an ethereal glow on Aris Thorne's weary face. He'd spent the last seventy-two hours hunched over the enigmatic book, its pages filled with symbols that defied easy categorization. They weren't hieroglyphs, nor cuneiform, nor any known alphabet. They were something else entirely – a visual language that seemed to resonate with the very fabric of space-time itself.

He'd contacted Dr. Lena Hanson, a leading expert in computational linguistics and AI at MIT. Lena, initially skeptical, had been captivated by the sheer strangeness of the symbols. Together, they'd developed a sophisticated AI program, dubbed "Chronos," designed to analyze the book's intricate patterns and potentially decipher its meaning. Chronos wasn't just a translator; it was a pattern-recognition engine, capable of identifying underlying structures in data that would escape human observation.

The initial results were frustratingly fragmented. Chronos identified recurring motifs, constellations of symbols that appeared in various combinations throughout the text. Some appeared to represent celestial bodies – stars, galaxies, nebulae – but the depiction was far from conventional. They weren't simple drawings; they were complex, multi-layered representations that seemed to encode additional information within their structure. The

AI struggled to contextualize these images, spitting out probabilistic interpretations that were as often misleading as they were insightful.

One recurring symbol, a spiral galaxy depicted with an unsettlingly accurate representation of its gravitational lensing effect, consistently appeared alongside a sequence of seemingly random numerical values. Lena, working remotely via a secure video link, hypothesized that these numbers might represent coordinates – perhaps celestial coordinates pinpointing specific locations in the universe.

"Aris," Lena said, her voice tight with excitement, "look at this. The numerical sequences... they're not random. There's a pattern, a subtle variation in the spacing, almost like a musical score."

Aris leaned closer to the screen. Chronos had overlaid the numerical sequences onto a graphical representation, and the result was startling. The numbers, when plotted against each other, formed a complex, three-dimensional waveform. It resembled a cosmic dance, a choreography of celestial movements unfolding across unimaginable scales of time and space.

Days blurred into nights. The Chilean desert wind howled outside, a relentless symphony of isolation mirroring the chaos churning within Aris's mind. He fueled himself on black coffee and the adrenaline of discovery, the pressure of the Obsidian Order's looming presence a constant undercurrent to his work. The fragmented translations were slowly coalescing into a narrative, though one that defied easy comprehension.

Chronos began to reveal a hidden layer of meaning within the text. Embedded within the primary symbolic language was a secondary code, a series of seemingly meaningless glyphs that appeared randomly interspersed throughout the pages. However, Lena discovered that these glyphs represented a different kind of information – a narrative, seemingly a history of the universe, told not through images, but through pure mathematical equations.

"It's... breathtaking," Lena breathed, her voice barely audible. "These aren't just equations; they're descriptions of fundamental forces, the evolution of spacetime, the birth and death of stars, the formation of galaxies. It's cosmology at a

level... we've only dreamed of."

The equations, deciphered by Chronos, were far beyond current human understanding. They described concepts that challenged the established models of astrophysics. They alluded to a universe far more complex, far more intricate, than anything Aris had ever imagined. It hinted at dimensions beyond our four-dimensional reality, forces beyond the known laws of physics, and a history of the cosmos shrouded in mystery.

The book, Aris realized, wasn't just a historical document; it was a blueprint. Its detailed processes and phenomena that could rewrite humanity's understanding of the universe's origin, evolution, and ultimate fate. It suggested the existence of advanced civilizations, capable of manipulating the fundamental fabric of reality, and technologies that defied his wildest scientific speculations.

One equation, in particular, stood out. It described a cataclysmic event, a cosmic upheaval that could have reshaped the universe. The equation, when modeled by Chronos, predicted a future event, a singular moment of cosmic rearrangement that would eclipse any previously recorded celestial occurrences. The timing, alarmingly, was within the next century.

But the book didn't just provide a theoretical description; it included schematics, diagrams depicting complex machinery – devices that seemed capable of manipulating gravity, time, and even space itself. These were not just theoretical concepts; they were practical plans, blueprints for technologies beyond anything currently conceived by humans.

The implications were staggering. This knowledge, if unleashed, could be humanity's salvation or its utter destruction. Aris felt a surge of cold dread. The Obsidian Order wasn't simply interested in suppressing this knowledge; they were probably trying to weaponize it.

The more Aris deciphered, the more he realized the terrifying truth – the book wasn't just a record of the past or a blueprint for the future, it was a key, a gateway to something far more profound. It was a manual for controlling the universe itself. The weight of this realization crashed down on him, heavier than any physical burden.

His work had gone beyond simple scientific investigation. It had become a race against time, a fight for the survival of humanity. He glanced at the secure video feed, seeing Lena's exhausted but determined face. They had only scratched the surface of the book's secrets. The deeper they delved, the greater the risks became. The Obsidian Order's shadow loomed large, but Aris was not alone. He had an ally, and together, they would face the cosmic storm that was brewing. The fight for the universe had begun, and it was a fight they could not afford to lose. The universe's fate, it seemed, rested on the fragile shoulders of a disgraced astrophysicist and a brilliant computational linguist, battling against a shadowy organization and the weight of cosmic secrets. The next revelation might bring triumph or utter annihilation. The only certainty was the relentless, unstoppable march of time.

The First Threat

The sleek, black vehicle materialized out of the desert night like a phantom, its presence only betrayed by the faint hum that vibrated through the dry earth. Dr. Aris Thorne, his heart hammering a frantic rhythm against his ribs, watched from his makeshift observatory, the stolen book clutched tightly to his chest. He'd known the risk, of course. The anomalies he'd detected in the cosmic microwave background radiation, the whispers of an unknown physics tucked within the ancient starlight – these were secrets some would kill for. He hadn't anticipated the ruthlessness of 'The Obsidian Order,' nor their technological prowess.

The vehicle, a design beyond anything he'd seen in classified military documents, deployed a squad of figures clad in obsidian-black armor. Their movements were precise, almost balletic, a stark contrast to the harsh, unforgiving landscape. They moved with a silent efficiency that spoke volumes about their training and the technology that augmented their capabilities. Dr. Thorne, a brilliant astrophysicist but hardly a soldier, felt a surge of cold dread. This wasn't a robbery; it was an extraction, swift, surgical, and utterly terrifying.

He knew the book was more than just a collection of ancient writings; it was a key, a gateway to understanding the universe in a way that defied current scientific paradigms. It spoke of a cosmology far beyond the Standard Model, hinting at dimensions curled up within the fabric of spacetime, energies that dwarfed even those unleashed at the heart of a supernova. The Obsidian Order's interest wasn't academic; their desire was far more sinister.

The lead figure, his armor gleaming under the starlight, approached the observatory. He moved with a predatory grace, his every step measured and deliberate. Thorne could see no visible weapons, but the aura of lethal potential emanated from him like heat from a dying star. He carried himself with an unsettling calm, a disconcerting lack of emotion in the face of potential confrontation. This was no ordinary mercenary group; this was an organization operating on a level far removed from conventional power structures.

"Dr. Thorne," the figure's voice, amplified by some unseen technology, resonated with a chilling clarity, devoid of any human warmth. "We advise you to comply. Resistance is futile."

Thorne didn't reply, his mind racing to devise an escape plan. His makeshift observatory, a converted shipping container, offered little in the way of defense. He considered his options: a desperate run, a fight he knew he wouldn't win, or a surrender that could lead to something far worse. He glanced down at the book, its ancient script a silent promise of unimaginable power and equally unimaginable danger.

The Obsidian Order agents fanned out, surrounding the observatory, their movements synchronized perfectly. They were not merely soldiers; they were precision instruments, each one a lethal cog in a well-oiled machine of clandestine operations. They were the epitome of silent efficiency, their actions a testament to years of rigorous training and technological augmentation. Thorne could almost feel the weight of their collective presence, a palpable sense of impending doom settling upon him like a shroud.

As one agent approached the shipping container, he raised his hand. A beam of light, almost invisible to the naked eye, shot out from his glove, scanning the structure. It was a sophisticated analysis tool, capable of detecting any weak points in the observatory's defenses. This was no mere attempt at a forceful entry; this was a systematic dismantling of his sanctuary. Thorne realized that even if he could fight them off, they could simply disable his shelter, rendering his efforts futile. This was a battle he couldn't win by conventional means.

The agent reported back to the leader, his voice a low hum in Thorne's ear, the result of advanced communication technology. The leader nodded, a slight movement barely perceptible, but its implications were devastating. His team had identified vulnerabilities in the observatory's construction. The structure, hastily assembled as it was, wasn't designed to withstand anything close to this level of technological assault.

The leader approached the container again, his voice resonating with a chilling patience. "We are not here to cause harm, Dr. Thorne. Merely to retrieve what is rightfully ours.

Hand over the book, and we shall ensure your safety."

Thorne knew that 'safety' was a relative term in their lexicon. He was facing an organization with resources and capabilities far beyond his comprehension. He had to buy himself time, to find a way to outmaneuver them. He decided on a desperate gamble.

"This book," he said, his voice trembling slightly, but betraying none of his fear, "This book contains knowledge that could reshape our understanding of the universe. To fall into the wrong hands... it could be catastrophic." He paused, watching the leader's expression carefully. Any flicker of uncertainty, any hint of doubt, would be his lifeline.

The leader's face remained impassive, giving nothing away. He was a master of deception, a silent predator perfectly adapted to his environment. Thorne knew he needed something more convincing. Something that would trigger a level of caution, a pause in their calculated advance.

He gestured towards the vast expanse of the desert sky, the glittering tapestry of stars stretching endlessly above them. "Do you know what lies beyond the observable universe? The book holds the answers. Answers that could lead to unimaginable power, power that could dwarf anything you currently possess." He paused, his words hanging in the night air, the silence punctuated only by the faint hum of the Obsidian Order's technology.

The leader finally spoke, his voice laced with a hint of something akin to curiosity, or possibly even interest. "And what is the price of this unimaginable power, Dr. Thorne? What are the consequences?" This was the opening he'd been waiting for, the slightest crack in their impenetrable facade.

Thorne had another desperate gamble in his arsenal. He knew of a hidden satellite, an experimental probe launched years ago, equipped with a highly advanced AI capable of disrupting even the most sophisticated systems. It was a long shot, but it was his only shot. He had to make them believe that releasing the information within the book would unleash something far more dangerous than they ever anticipated. He would need to convince them that their gain is far outweighed by the risk.

"The price," he said, his voice low and intense, "is far greater than you can comprehend. The book speaks of cosmic entities, forces that exist beyond our current understanding. Unleashing their power could unravel the very fabric of reality. You would be unleashing forces far beyond your ability to control." He held their gaze, letting the gravity of his words hang in the air. He knew he was pushing their limits of patience and trust, his every word carrying the weight of life and death.

The leader remained silent for a long, excruciating moment, his eyes scanning Thorne's face, attempting to gauge the truth behind his words. The tension was palpable, heavy enough to choke the breath from Thorne's lungs. The outcome hung precariously in the balance. The fate of the universe, it seemed, depended on the Obsidian Order's decision – a decision based not on brute force, but on a calculated assessment of risk and reward, a precarious dance on the edge of the precipice of reality itself. The silence stretched, a terrifying eternity.

Seeking Allies

The Obsidian Order's leader finally spoke, his voice a low, gravelly rumble that resonated with an unnerving calm. "You claim this book holds the key to... altering reality?"

Thorne swallowed hard, his throat suddenly dry. "Yes. It speaks of a fundamental force, a pre-Big Bang energy, a... a cosmic architect, if you will. Its manipulation could rewrite the universe's fundamental laws."

A flicker of something akin to interest, or perhaps skepticism, crossed the leader's face. "And you believe you can control this... architect?"

"No," Thorne admitted, the words escaping in a shaky breath. "But understanding it... that's the first step. Preventing its misuse is the crucial part. The book... it's incomplete. Fragments of knowledge are scattered throughout, hinting at a vast, intricate cosmology." He risked a glance at the book resting on the passenger seat. "The Order... you have resources I lack. Ancient texts, decryption technology, access to..." he hesitated, "...to places and people I could only dream of reaching."

The leader's gaze remained intense. "And what is your offer, Dr. Thorne? To willingly deliver yourself into our hands, a pawn in our grand design?"

Thorne took a deep breath, the desert air stinging his lungs. "Not a pawn," he countered, "an ally. A collaboration. I offer my expertise in astrophysics, my knowledge of the anomalies I've discovered. In return, I request your resources, your expertise in deciphering ancient languages, in cryptography... in understanding the potential implications of what this book reveals. I need to understand this force before it falls into the wrong hands."

The silence that followed was less tense than before, more of a weighing of probabilities. The leader considered Thorne, the book, and the potential consequences, the cosmic balance hanging in the precarious balance. Finally, a nod. "Very well, Dr. Thorne. Your audacity is... refreshing. We'll consider this a... temporary alliance. But failure will have consequences far beyond what you can comprehend."

The black vehicle sped away, leaving Thorne alone in the vast emptiness of the desert, the hum of the vehicle fading into the wind. He had survived, but the sense of relief was fleeting, replaced by a heavy weight of responsibility. He needed help, someone who understood ancient languages, someone who could decipher the cryptic symbology within the book. His mind went to Lena Hanson, a former colleague, a brilliant linguist and cryptographer who had always been fascinated by the intersection of language and cosmology. Lena had scoffed at his theory's years ago, but she also possessed an undeniable brilliance. He needed her.

He reached his small, sparsely furnished apartment in the city's outskirts, the city lights a distant, glittering backdrop to his own private struggle. The place reflected his current circumstances, scattered papers, half-finished equations scribbled on whiteboards, books stacked precariously. The stolen book, a heavy weight in its leather binding, sat on his desk, the enigma radiating an almost palpable energy. He pulled out his phone, his fingers trembling slightly as he dialed Lena's number.

She answered on the third ring, her voice laced with a cautious reserve. "Aris? What is it? It's three in the morning."

"Lena, I need your help. I've... I've discovered something extraordinary. Something that could change everything."

Lena's voice sharpened. "Aris, I know you've been working on those... unconventional theories. I'm not sure I understand what you mean by 'extraordinary.'"

Thorne hesitated, unsure how much to reveal. "It's more than just theories, Lena. It's... evidence. Concrete evidence. I

need to show you something."

He could almost sense her skepticism through the phone, but her voice retained a hint of curiosity. "What kind of

evidence?"

"A book," Thorne replied, his voice hoarse. "An ancient book... with the potential to rewrite our understanding of the

universe. And some very powerful people are already after it."

Lena fell silent for a moment, before a low whistle escaped her lips. "Aris, you're not making any sense."

"I know, it sounds crazy. But you're the only one I can trust. Meet me in an hour at the old observatory. Bring your decryption tools. Bring anything you have that can help us decode ancient languages, especially those related to

cosmology."

The appointment was made under the cloak of the city's night. Lena arrived, her face etched with a mix of apprehension and intrigue. She had changed, he saw: sharper, more determined, her eyes reflecting the city lights. The years of academia had done nothing to dull the intensity in her gaze. She carried a battered briefcase, inside of which Thorne knew lay a treasure trove of technological tools, the key to unlocking this book's secrets.

The observatory was a refuge, cold and quiet except for the hum of the old equipment. Thorne showed Lena the book, the weight of its secrets palpable as he placed it in her hands. The cover was worn, the leather cracked with age, the script on the cover intricate and alien. It was a language neither of them recognized, but Lena's eyes shone with a familiar spark of scientific determination.

"This..." she breathed, tracing a finger across the cryptic symbols. "This is unlike anything I've ever seen. It's a combination of mathematical notation and what looks like... Sumerian cuneiform, but warped, distorted, almost as if it's

been passed through some kind of... cosmic filter."

They began their work, a silent partnership fueled by adrenaline and the weight of the untold consequences of failure. Lena's expertise in cryptography and ancient languages combined with Thorne's knowledge of cosmology proved to be a powerful synergy. They worked for hours, piecing together fragments, deciphering encoded messages, translating cryptic passages. The book spoke not only of a fundamental pre-Big Bang energy, but also of a vast, interdimensional conspiracy – a hidden history of the universe that had been meticulously concealed for millennia.

As they delved deeper, a chilling realization dawned upon them. The Obsidian Order wasn't just a secretive organization; it was a direct descendant of an ancient civilization, a civilization that had possessed and understood the power described within the book. They had used it – for purposes that were both terrifying and incomprehensible. The book hinted at a catastrophic event in the universe's distant past, an event directly linked to the misuse of this fundamental force. The Order's current actions were a mere echo, a desperate attempt to reignite that catastrophic power.

As dawn broke, painting the sky in hues of orange and pink, a chilling image materialized from the coded descriptions within the book: a map. Not of a physical location, but of a celestial alignment, a precise configuration of stars and galaxies. A cosmic key, it seemed, to accessing this primeval energy. The alignment was approaching, and it was imminent.

With a growing sense of dread, Thorne and Lena realized the stakes were far higher than they had initially imagined. This wasn't just about understanding the universe; it was about preventing its destruction. They were far from safe. The Obsidian Order was already closing in, their reach far greater than Thorne had ever imagined. Their fragile alliance, born in the desperate hope of preventing a cosmic catastrophe, was about to face its first true test. The race against time had begun. The fate of the universe, it seemed, now rested on the shoulders of two unlikely allies, bound together by a book of ancient secrets and the terrifying knowledge it revealed.

Unraveling the Conspiracies Clues

The flickering holographic projection cast an ethereal glow across Thorne's face, highlighting the deep lines of exhaustion etched around his eyes. Lena Hanson, her expression equally strained, leaned closer, her breath misting in the cool air of the hidden research lab. The translated fragments of the ancient text, painstakingly deciphered over the past few days, shimmered before them, a chaotic tapestry woven from symbols that defied easy comprehension. Yet, within that chaos, patterns were beginning to emerge.

The initial translations, while fragmented, hinted at a cataclysmic event – a cosmic collision of unimaginable scale – that occurred millennia ago, predating even the earliest known human civilizations. The text referred to it as "The Great Fracture," a disruption in the fabric of spacetime that sent ripples across the cosmos. But what was most unsettling was the implication that the Obsidian Order possessed knowledge, a detailed understanding, of this event, knowledge not accessible through any known scientific means.

"They knew," Thorne murmured, his voice barely audible above the hum of the ventilation system. "They knew about The Great Fracture, and they've been preparing for something..."

Lena shivered, not entirely from the cold. "Preparing for what? Another Fracture? Or... something else entirely?"

The text fragments alluded to a civilization that had existed long before humanity, a civilization so advanced that their technology dwarfed even the wildest imaginings of modern science. This civilization, the translations suggested, had foreseen The Great Fracture, possessing the capability to not only predict it but to potentially manipulate the very fabric of spacetime itself. The Obsidian Order, according to the fragmented narratives, was somehow connected to this lost civilization, either as its direct descendants or as custodians of its legacy. The implications sent a chill down Thorne's spine. He felt the weight of an unimaginable burden, the weight of knowledge that could shatter the foundations of human understanding.

The next few days were a blur of intense research, fueled by caffeine and a desperate need to understand the scope of the conspiracy. Thorne and Lena worked tirelessly, poring over the translated texts, comparing them to astronomical data, searching for any corroborating evidence. They cross-referenced the ancient astronomical notations with modern star charts, analyzing celestial alignments and comparing them to the cryptic descriptions of the "Great Fracture" within the ancient texts. They found anomalies – subtle inconsistencies in galactic formations, gravitational distortions that didn't align with current cosmological models. These anomalies, invisible to the untrained eye, suggested a distortion of space-time that echoed the events described in the ancient book.

Their research led them to the study of dark matter and dark energy – the mysterious, unseen forces that constitute the vast majority of the universe's mass-energy density. The ancient texts hinted at the manipulation of these forces, suggesting a level of technological mastery beyond human comprehension. The implications were staggering. If the Obsidian Order possessed the ability to manipulate dark matter and dark energy, they could literally rewrite the laws of physics, potentially creating or destroying entire universes.

As they delved deeper, Thorne and Lena uncovered a series of coded messages within the text – intricate patterns hidden within the seemingly random symbols. They employed advanced decryption algorithms, pushing the limits of their computational resources. The decrypted messages revealed a network of clandestine Obsidian Order operations across the

globe, hidden in plain sight. Research facilities masquerading as universities, astronomical observatories acting as fronts for secret experiments, and seemingly innocuous corporations serving as conduits for resources and personnel. The scale of their operation was breathtaking, a vast conspiracy spanning centuries, meticulously concealed within the fabric of human society.

Thorne, a man accustomed to dealing with the vastness of the cosmos, found himself overwhelmed by the sheer audacity of the Obsidian Order's plan. It wasn't simply about power or wealth; it was about controlling the very essence of existence. The possibility of a technologically advanced civilization capable of altering the very fabric of spacetime was terrifying, and its implications were far-reaching.

One of the decoded messages referred to a specific celestial event, a predicted alignment of several galaxies that was due to occur in the coming months. This alignment, according to the text, was pivotal to the Obsidian Order's plans – the catalyst for an event of unimaginable consequence. But the nature of this event remained cryptic, shrouded in veiled language and esoteric symbolism. Thorne and Lena speculated it might be a repeat of the "Great Fracture," but on a scale far exceeding the original, potentially leading to the unraveling of the universe as they knew it.

As they pieced together the fragments of the conspiracy, they also began to uncover the true nature of the Obsidian Order's ambition. Their goal wasn't simply domination or control; it was something far more profound, something that threatened the very foundation of reality. The decoded messages hinted at an attempt to reshape the universe itself, to redefine the fundamental constants of nature, to create a new reality tailored to their own twisted vision.

The longer they investigated, the more they realized they weren't dealing with a mere conspiracy, but with an existential threat to the very fabric of existence. The weight of this realization settled heavily on their shoulders. They were no longer simply scientists unraveling an ancient mystery; they were guardians of reality, tasked with preventing an unimaginable cosmic catastrophe. Their fragile alliance, initially built on shared curiosity and a mutual distrust, was solidifying into a resolute partnership forged in the crucible of a shared destiny.

The decoded messages also revealed the Obsidian Order's surprising connection to various seemingly unrelated global events – from unexplained energy surges to unusual gravitational anomalies that had been dismissed as natural phenomena. Thorne and Lena, drawing on their expertise in astrophysics and cosmology, were able to show a subtle correlation between these seemingly unconnected events. These anomalies, they realized, were not random occurrences; they were carefully orchestrated, subtle manipulations of spacetime itself – subtle ripples in the fabric of reality caused by the Obsidian Order's clandestine operations.

The more they learned, the more terrifying the Obsidian Order became. They were not merely a powerful organization; they were a cosmic force, wielding powers that defied human understanding and threatening to unravel the very fabric of reality. Their influence reached into the

highest echelons of power, their tentacles entwined with governments, corporations, and scientific institutions. The realization that their reach extended this far, and had for so long, filled Thorne and Lena with a sense of profound unease. They were facing an enemy that was not only powerful but also deeply embedded within the very structure of the world.

The weight of their discovery, the enormity of the task ahead, pressed down on them. The fate of the universe, it seemed, rested on their shoulders. They had to expose the Obsidian Order, expose their plans before it was too late. But the organization had been operating in the shadows for millennia, and their reach was far beyond anything Thorne or Lena had ever encountered. The task before them was daunting, a perilous journey into the heart of a conspiracy that threatened the very essence of existence. The next move was crucial; a wrong step could trigger the apocalypse they were desperately trying to prevent. The ticking clock of the cosmic alignment loomed ever closer, a constant reminder of the limited time they had. The race had begun, and they were far from the finish line.

The Books Revelation of Dark Matter

The flickering holographic projection cast eerie shadows across Dr. Aris Thorne's face, the symbols from the ancient book swirling like nebulae. Lena Hanson, her brow furrowed in concentration, adjusted the parameters on her console. "The translation is... unsettling," she whispered, her voice barely audible above the hum of the sophisticated decryption equipment. For weeks, they had been painstakingly deciphering the book's cryptic script, a language that seemed to defy linguistic conventions, yet hinted at a profound understanding of the universe's deepest secrets.

The breakthrough came unexpectedly, not in a burst of clear, concise language, but in a series of fragmented images and complex mathematical equations that, when pieced together, painted a picture far beyond their wildest imaginings. The book didn't simply describe dark matter; it revealed its sentience. It wasn't a passive constituent of the cosmos, a silent observer in the grand cosmic ballet; it was an active participant, a force with its own consciousness, its own agenda, its own will.

The equations illustrated a complex network of interactions between dark matter and other forms of energy, a web of influence that stretched across the vast expanse of the universe. It wasn't just gravity that held galaxies together; it was the subtle manipulation of dark matter, a cosmic puppet master pulling strings across light-years. The images depicted swirling patterns of energy, complex geometries that pulsed with an almost biological rhythm, hinting at a structure, an organization, a society of dark matter entities far beyond human comprehension.

"It's...alive," Thorne breathed, his voice filled with a mixture of awe and apprehension. He had spent years studying the cold, indifferent equations of astrophysics, but this was different. This was a revelation that shattered his previously held beliefs about the universe's fundamental nature, challenging everything he thought he knew. The cosmos, he realized, was far more complex, far more alive, and far more terrifying than he could have ever imagined.

Hanson, equally shocked, ran her hand through her hair, her eyes wide with disbelief. "But...how? How can something

so fundamental, so pervasive, be sentient?"

The book offered few answers, its cryptic pronouncements shrouded in allegory and metaphor. It spoke of a "Great Consciousness," a collective entity woven from the fabric of dark matter itself, an ancient being that had shaped the universe, not through brute force, but through subtle manipulation and guidance. It described a history of the universe, not as a random sequence of events, but as a carefully orchestrated symphony of cosmic forces, orchestrated by this very same Great Consciousness.

The implication was staggering: the universe wasn't simply a cold, indifferent void, but a carefully crafted creation, a living entity in its own right. And this entity, this Great Consciousness of dark matter, was not necessarily benevolent. The book hinted at a complex interplay between dark matter and dark energy, suggesting that the accelerated expansion of the universe was not merely a natural phenomenon, but a deliberate act, a cosmic project driven by the will of this enigmatic entity.

The more they deciphered, the more unsettling the revelation became. The book spoke of "Guardians," entities within the dark matter network responsible for maintaining the delicate balance of the universe. These Guardians, it implied, had observed humanity's development for millennia, silently watching as civilization rose and fell, their patience seemingly endless. But their patience, the book suggested, was not infinite.

The text then shifted, abruptly changing from descriptions of cosmic processes to warnings. It spoke of a "Dissonance," an imbalance in the cosmic order caused by humanity's reckless exploitation of resources and the careless disruption of the natural equilibrium. The

Guardians, it seemed, were growing increasingly concerned. The book suggested that humanity's actions were not only threatening its own survival, but also the very fabric of the universe.

The implications were terrifying. If the universe was indeed sentient, and if humanity was perceived as a threat, what would the response be? Would the universe simply shrug off the insignificant specks of life on a small, pale blue planet? Or would it take action, a corrective measure to restore the cosmic balance, even if it meant eradicating humanity in the process?

This question haunted Thorne and Hanson as they continued to decode the ancient book. They were no longer just dealing with a scientific mystery; they were confronting an existential threat, a cosmic judgment that could determine the fate of humanity itself. The universe was not merely a stage for humanity's drama; it was a living entity with its own agency, its own will, and its own deeply unsettling plans.

The book also offered a glimpse into the Obsidian Order's motives. They were not merely a shadowy organization seeking power; they were attempting to manipulate the very fabric of existence, to harness the power of dark matter for their own nefarious purposes. The text suggested that they had been studying the ancient book for centuries, piecing together its cryptic clues, seeking to unlock the secrets of the Great Consciousness and bend it to their will. Their goal, it appeared, was not merely dominion over Earth, but control over the universe itself.

The implications were horrifying. If the Obsidian Order succeeded, it could unleash a cosmic catastrophe of unimaginable proportions, a disruption of the universe's delicate equilibrium that could lead to its collapse. The very fabric of reality, it seemed, was at stake. Thorne and Hanson were not just fighting for the survival of humanity; they were fighting for the survival of the universe itself. The weight of this realization pressed down on them, heavy as a black hole. The race against time had begun, and the stakes were higher than either of them had ever imagined. They were dealing with not just a conspiracy, but a cosmic conspiracy, one that could extinguish the very stars themselves. The book's final coded message flashed across the screen, a chilling warning, a final countdown to a cosmic reckoning.

The Nature of Dark Energy

The holographic projection shimmered, the cryptic symbols resolving into a series of complex equations. Lena ran a hand through her already disheveled hair, her eyes tracing the lines of arcane mathematics that seemed both alien and strangely familiar. "It's...a cosmological model," she breathed, her voice hushed with awe and apprehension. "But unlike anything we've ever encountered."

Dr. Thorne leaned closer, his gaze intense. He had spent decades studying the universe, pushing the boundaries of astrophysical understanding, yet this ancient text was revealing a cosmology that challenged everything he thought he knew. The equations described not just the expansion of the universe, but its acceleration, a phenomenon attributed to dark energy, the enigmatic force that makes up 68% of the universe's composition, yet remains stubbornly elusive to direct observation.

"The book... it's not just describing dark energy," Thorne murmured, his finger tracing a particularly intricate sequence of symbols. "It's describing its manipulation. Its control."

The equations suggested a level of sophistication far beyond human comprehension. They indicated a manipulation of the cosmological constant, the parameter that governs the universe's expansion rate. The ancient civilization that authored this text had not simply understood dark energy; they had mastered it. They were, according to the text, capable of influencing its effects, slowing or accelerating the expansion of the universe at will. This was not merely theoretical physics; it was cosmic engineering.

The implications were staggering. The universe's expansion, previously understood as a relatively passive process driven by the initial conditions of the Big Bang, was now revealed as something far more dynamic, potentially guided, manipulated, even weaponized. The very fabric of spacetime, the foundation of existence itself, seemed to be under the influence of an unseen force, a force that, according to this ancient text, had been consciously wielded by a civilization that had vanished from the cosmos eons ago.

Lena's fingers danced across her console, running simulations based on the equations. The results were horrifying. A small alteration to the cosmological constant, a minuscule shift in the dark energy's influence, could trigger catastrophic consequences. The accelerated expansion could become runaway expansion, ripping apart galaxies, stars, even atoms themselves in a cosmic "Big Rip". Conversely, a reduction in dark energy could cause the universe's expansion to halt, leading to a "Big Crunch," a catastrophic collapse back into a singularity, a reversal of the Big Bang. The ancient text hinted at both possibilities, presenting them not as natural occurrences, but as deliberate actions, potentially used as weapons in a cosmic war of unimaginable scale.

"The Obsidian Order," Thorne muttered, the name a chilling echo in the silent laboratory. "They weren't just after this book for its historical significance, or even for its technological secrets. They were after the power it described."

The ancient text didn't explicitly state the nature of dark energy, but it offered glimpses into its fundamental properties. It suggested that dark energy was not simply a uniform force permeating spacetime, but possessed a structure, a network of interconnected nodes that could be influenced, manipulated, even controlled. It was a cosmic infrastructure, invisible yet vast, holding the universe together—or tearing it apart—depending on who controlled its levers.

The book contained not just equations, but diagrams, intricate three-dimensional representations of this dark energy network, a cosmic web of unimaginable complexity. The diagrams showed pathways, nodes, and conduits, suggesting the existence of a cosmic infrastructure, much like a vast network of superhighways crisscrossing the universe. It was a frightening thought; the universe, in its entirety, potentially governed by an invisible, controllable system.

"Think of it like this," Thorne explained, gesturing towards the holographic projection, "Imagine the universe as a giant, expanding balloon. Dark energy is the air inside, pushing it outwards. But the equations suggest this 'air' isn't uniform; it's structured, controlled. The Obsidian Order wants to control the air pressure, to decide whether the balloon

expands until it bursts, or contracts until it collapses."

Lena paled. "And they're close," she whispered, her eyes fixed on the screen displaying the simulations. "Their technology... it's based on the same principles. They're trying to build their own control mechanism, to replicate what the ancient civilization achieved."

The implications were terrifying. If the Obsidian Order succeeded, they could not only control the fate of the universe, they could wield it as a weapon. They could trigger a Big Rip or a Big Crunch, extinguishing all life, unraveling the very fabric of reality. The universe, it seemed, was not simply expanding; it was being manipulated, and humanity was caught in the crossfire.

The ancient text offered further insights into the nature of dark energy, describing it as a form of "negative mass energy," a concept that defied conventional physics. Negative mass-energy, according to the text, possessed properties that inverted conventional gravitational forces, creating repulsive gravity, the driving force behind the universe's accelerated expansion. It wasn't just pushing the universe apart; it was actively working against its own collapse, maintaining a delicate balance between expansion and contraction.

The book detailed the risks involved in manipulating such a potent force. It described potential feedback loops, catastrophic chain reactions that could destabilize the universe's delicate equilibrium, leading to unpredictable and potentially devastating consequences. The ancient civilization, the text implied, had paid a terrible price for their mastery over dark energy, their hubris leading to their own demise. The text served as a chilling warning, a cautionary tale of scientific overreach, a testament to the dangers of meddling with forces beyond human comprehension.

The text also hinted at other dimensions, extra spatial dimensions that interacted with our own through dark energy, suggesting the existence of a greater cosmic network connecting various universes, or perhaps even alternate realities. These interactions, according to the book, could be harnessed to achieve unimaginable feats, but also posed existential risks. It was a cosmic tapestry, woven from threads of space, time, and dark energy, a reality far more complex and dangerous than even the most visionary scientists could have imagined.

Thorne and Lena, armed with this newfound knowledge, realized the sheer magnitude of their task. They were not just fighting a conspiracy; they were fighting to protect the universe itself. The Obsidian Order was not just after power; they were after the power to control existence, the power to rewrite the very laws of physics. The race against time was on. Each passing moment brought them closer to a cosmic precipice, a point of no return where the fate of the universe would be decided, not by natural laws, but by the machinations of a shadowy organization wielding a force far more powerful than any weapon humanity could ever conceive. The weight of this responsibility pressed down upon them, heavier than any black hole, driving them forward in their desperate attempt to unravel the mysteries of dark energy and prevent a cosmic catastrophe. The very fabric of reality, it seemed, was in their hands.

The Obsidian Orders Motives

The holographic projection flickered, the equations now shifting, morphing into a three-dimensional representation of a galactic structure. It wasn't a typical spiral or elliptical galaxy; this was something... different. The model pulsed with an inner light, a luminosity that Thorne recognized as emanating not from stars, but from something far more fundamental, something far more... unsettling.

"Dark energy," Lena whispered, her finger tracing the luminous tendrils weaving through the simulated galaxy. "It's... being manipulated. Look at the gravitational distortions."

Thorne leaned closer, his breath fogging the cool glass of the projection screen. The gravitational lensing effects depicted were extreme, defying any known natural phenomenon. Galaxies were being warped, stretched, and twisted into grotesque shapes, as if an unseen hand were playing with cosmic clay. "They're not just studying dark energy," he murmured, his voice tight with dawning horror. "They're

controlling it. Weaponizing it."

Hanson, who had remained relatively silent until now, spoke, his voice grave. "The equations... they suggest a method of harnessing dark energy's repulsive force, using it to... to alter spacetime itself." He paused, swallowing hard. "Think about it: manipulating the expansion rate of the universe. Creating localized gravitational anomalies. Causing... singularities."

The implications were staggering. The Obsidian Order wasn't just interested in understanding the universe's deepest mysteries; they were attempting to rewrite its fundamental laws. They were playing God, and the stakes were not just planetary, but cosmic. The potential for destruction was beyond comprehension.

"But why?" Lena asked, her voice laced with disbelief.

"What could possibly motivate them to wield such power?

What could they possibly hope to gain?"

Thorne ran a hand through his hair, his mind racing to find an answer. The sheer scale of the Obsidian Order's ambition was almost incomprehensible. Was it mere conquest, a desire for absolute power over all of existence? Or was there something more insidious at play, some hidden agenda beyond the naked lust for domination?

Hanson, ever the pragmatist, pointed to a section of the holographic projection, a cluster of seemingly random symbols nestled within the complex equations. "This... this appears to be a key. A decryption key, perhaps. It's tied directly to the manipulation of dark energy, but it's... fragmented. It's as if they're not even completely in control of the process themselves."

The fragmented nature of the key suggested a possible vulnerability. Perhaps the Obsidian Order wasn't as omnipotent as they initially appeared. Perhaps their control over dark energy was not absolute, but rather precarious, dependent on this elusive key.

"If we can decipher this," Lena said, her voice regaining its strength, "we might find a way to disrupt their plans, to counter their manipulation of dark energy."

The next few days were a blur of frantic research. Thorne,

Lena, and Hanson poured over the fragmented data, deciphering the cryptic symbols, cross-referencing them with every cosmological model and mathematical equation they could find. They worked tirelessly, fueled by adrenaline and the sheer weight of their responsibility, driven by the terrifying understanding of what the Obsidian Order was capable of.

The key, they discovered, wasn't just a simple cryptographic code; it was a complex algorithm, interwoven with principles of quantum mechanics and string theory. It involved manipulating the fundamental forces of nature, something far beyond the capabilities of current technology. Yet, embedded within the algorithm, they found hints of a weakness, a flaw in the Obsidian Order's methodology.

The Order, it seemed, was attempting to exploit a loophole in the universe's fundamental laws, a subtle imbalance in the interplay of dark energy and dark matter. They were trying to achieve a state of cosmic imbalance, using dark energy as a lever to warp spacetime and reshape the very fabric of reality according to their twisted will. But their approach was crude, violent, and potentially unstable. Their algorithm, while powerful, was inherently flawed, prone to catastrophic failures.

Thorne realized the Obsidian Order's ambitions went far beyond mere control; they sought a complete restructuring of reality, a cosmic makeover that would potentially obliterate all existing forms of life and reshape the universe in their own distorted image. The very notion sent chills down his spine. This wasn't just about power; it was about cosmic creation and destruction, a warped ambition exceeding mere planetary domination.

Their research uncovered further evidence of the Order's activities. They had established covert facilities throughout the globe, hidden deep underground, shielded from detection. These facilities were not merely research labs; they were enormous, clandestine machines, designed to channel and amplify the power of dark energy, to bend space and time according to their commands.

The scale of the operation was breathtaking, terrifying in its audacity. The Obsidian Order was not a small group of fanatics; they were a vast, well-organized network operating on a global scale, with seemingly limitless resources at their disposal. Their influence extended to governments, corporations, and even scientific institutions. The entire world, it seemed, was unknowingly caught in their web.

The deeper they delved, the more disturbing the truth became. The Order's goal wasn't just to control dark energy; it was to understand and exploit its connection to dark matter, to harness the combined power of these mysterious forces to achieve a level of cosmic domination never before imagined. They were attempting to create a new universe, a universe entirely under their control, a universe shaped in their image.

Their research also revealed the Order's surprisingly complex internal structure. It wasn't simply a hierarchical organization; it resembled more of a hive mind, with individual members connected through a network of shared consciousness, their minds linked through a complex technological system yet to be fully understood. This collective consciousness amplified their abilities, allowing them to coordinate their actions with unsettling precision. It was a terrifying vision of future technology, a symbiotic fusion of technology and consciousness beyond human understanding.

The flaw in their algorithm, however, offered a sliver of hope. If Thorne, Lena, and Hanson could exploit this flaw, they could potentially disrupt the Order's plans, causing a catastrophic chain reaction within the dark energy manipulation process. It was a risky gambit, a desperate long-shot, but it was their only chance. The fate of the universe rested on their ability to decipher the remaining fragments of the key and successfully implement their counter-measure. The weight of their task pressed down upon them, a crushing burden only slightly mitigated by the knowledge that the universe itself depended on their success. They were not just scientists anymore; they were the universe's last defense, tasked with preventing a cosmic apocalypse of unimaginable scale. The countdown had begun.

A Race Against Time

The holographic galaxy pulsed, its ethereal light casting an eerie glow on the three faces illuminated by its otherworldly radiance. Thorne, Lena, and Hanson, three scientists thrust into a cosmic drama far beyond their wildest imaginings, stared at the projection, the implications of what they saw sinking in with terrifying clarity. The Obsidian Order wasn't simply studying dark energy; they were weaponizing it. Their manipulation wasn't subtle; it was a brute-force assault on the fundamental fabric of spacetime, a cosmic vandalism of unimaginable scale.

The flawed algorithm, initially a source of frustration, now appeared as a potential lifeline. It was a weakness in the Order's carefully crafted system, a chink in their otherwise impenetrable armor. Exploiting this flaw, however, was akin to defusing a bomb while it was already detonating. One wrong move, one miscalculation, and the universe could be irrevocably altered, possibly annihilated.

"The key," Lena whispered, her voice barely audible above the hum of the supercomputer, "it's not just a code; it's a counter-measure. A way to disrupt their process, to overload their system."

Hanson, the pragmatic engineer of the group, ran a hand through his already disheveled hair. "But how? The key is fragmented, incomplete. We're working with scraps of information, trying to build a functional counter-measure from theoretical physics."

Thorne, the theoretical physicist, leaned forward, his eyes fixated on the shifting holographic projections. "The fragments... they're not random. They're clues. Each piece offers a glimpse into the Order's methodology, revealing the underlying structure of their manipulation. We need to assemble these clues, to understand the pattern, before it's too late."

The pressure was immense. They were racing against an unseen clock, a cosmic deadline they couldn't even begin to quantify. Each passing moment brought them closer to an unimaginable catastrophe, a universe reshaped by the Obsidian Order's malevolent intent. The weight of their responsibility pressed heavily on them, the potential for failure a constant, chilling presence.

Their work was a delicate dance between theoretical physics and cutting-edge technology. They poured over the fragmented data, piecing together the intricate puzzle with painstaking precision. Lena, a master coder, worked tirelessly, translating Thorne's theoretical insights into executable algorithms. Hanson, with his engineering expertise, ensured the supercomputer could handle the immense computational load required for such an ambitious task.

Days blurred into nights, the line between sleep and work dissolving into a haze of caffeine and adrenaline. The team functioned on minimal sustenance, driven by a shared sense of urgency, a desperate hope against impossible odds. The air in the lab crackled with tension, punctuated by the rhythmic whirring of the servers and the frantic typing of keyboards.

But their progress wasn't linear. They encountered roadblocks, dead ends, moments where the fragmented data seemed to lead to utter chaos. The frustration was palpable, threatening to overwhelm their resolve. There were arguments, moments of despair, the nagging doubt that their efforts were futile. Yet, they persevered, driven by the knowledge that the universe depended on their success.

Then, a breakthrough. Lena spotted a pattern in the data, a subtle repetition previously overlooked. It was a sequence of quantum numbers, seemingly insignificant on their own, yet when combined with other fragments, revealed a deeper meaning. It was a precise mathematical formula, describing a wave function capable of disrupting the Order's dark energy manipulation.

"This... this is it," Lena exclaimed, her voice trembling with a mixture of excitement and apprehension. "This formula can create a counter-wave, a disruptive force that could overload their system."

Hanson immediately began adapting the formula into code, translating Lena's discovery into a functional algorithm. The task was incredibly complex, demanding unparalleled precision and an intimate understanding of both quantum physics and advanced computer science. He worked with meticulous care, every line of code scrutinized, every calculation double-checked. The pressure was immense, but his resolve was unbreakable.

Meanwhile, Thorne delved deeper into the theoretical implications of Lena's discovery. He needed to understand the potential consequences, to anticipate any unforeseen problems. The counter-wave, while capable of disrupting the Order's actions, could also have unintended consequences. He had to ensure that their intervention didn't create a worse calamity.

As they worked, the holographic galaxy pulsed faster, its inner light intensifying. They could feel the Obsidian Order's influence growing stronger, their manipulation of dark energy accelerating. Time was running out, each passing second increasing the risk of catastrophic failure.

The final piece of the puzzle fell into place when Hanson successfully compiled the code. It was a complex algorithm, a symphony of computational instructions designed to unleash a targeted counter-wave capable of disrupting the Order's actions. The moment of truth had arrived.

Their hearts pounded in their chests as they initiated the program. The supercomputer hummed, its processors straining under the immense computational burden. The holographic galaxy pulsed violently, its ethereal glow fluctuating wildly. They watched, breathless, as the counterwave propagated through the simulated universe.

Initially, nothing seemed to happen. The suspense was agonizing, the silence deafening. Then, a subtle shift. The chaotic energy within the holographic galaxy began to stabilize, the wild fluctuations gradually diminishing. The counter-wave was working.

The pressure didn't subside immediately. The process was a delicate dance of energy manipulation, with unpredictable consequences possible at any point. There were moments when the system nearly collapsed, their hearts leaping into their throats. But they held on, their combined expertise and resolve pushing them forward.

Finally, after what seemed like an eternity, the holographic galaxy settled. The inner light dimmed, its pulsating glow replaced by a quiet, steady luminescence. The Obsidian Order's dark energy manipulation had been disrupted. They had won, at least for now.

The relief was immense, the exhaustion overwhelming. They had stared into the abyss and pulled back, defying the impossible, saving the universe from an unimaginable fate. But their victory was fragile, a temporary reprieve in a cosmic war far from over. The Obsidian Order was still out there, and the knowledge they possessed was a dangerous weapon in the wrong hands. Their race against time wasn't over; it had merely entered a new, more perilous phase.

Betrayal Within

The silence in the makeshift lab, carved into the bowels of the abandoned Kepler observatory, was thick enough to choke on. The holographic galaxy, a mesmerizing display of celestial chaos only moments before, had been deactivated, leaving behind an unsettling darkness punctuated only by the hum of cooling servers and the ragged breaths of the three scientists. Thorne, his face etched with a weariness that went beyond physical exhaustion, ran a hand through his already disheveled hair. Lena, ever the pragmatist, meticulously checked the encryption on their data logs, her movements precise and economical. Hanson, however, sat slumped in a chair, his usual jovial demeanor replaced by a haunted stillness.

The euphoria of their near-escape had evaporated, leaving behind a bitter residue of suspicion. The Obsidian Order's audacious plan to weaponize dark energy, their casual disregard for the fate of the universe, had shaken them to their core. But a new terror had crept in, a cold, insidious fear that gnawed at the edges of their hard-won victory. The breach in their security, the near-catastrophic failure of their counter-measure, hinted at something far more sinister than just a lapse in protocol. Someone within their small, tightly knit team had betrayed them.

"It wasn't a simple hack," Lena said, her voice low, breaking the silence. She tapped a sequence of numbers on her tablet, the screen glowing faintly in the dim light. "The Obsidian Order had access to our internal communication protocols, our encrypted files... they knew exactly what we were doing,

when we were doing it. They anticipated our every move." Thorne nodded, his eyes narrowed. "This wasn't just a data breach; it was an inside job. Someone fed them information, gave them the blueprint to our counter-measure. Someone we trusted."

The accusation hung heavy in the air, unspoken yet palpable. The three of them had shared a deep bond forged in the crucible of their shared peril. Yet, that very bond was now a source of profound vulnerability. Each glance, each hesitant word, was laden with suspicion. The comfortable camaraderie they had shared just hours before had shattered, replaced by a chilling uncertainty.

Hanson looked up, his eyes wide with a mixture of fear and disbelief. "It can't be... who? Who would do such a thing?"

The question hung unanswered, a dark cloud looming over them. They had only each other, and now, that trust had been irrevocably fractured. The implications were devastating. Their ability to fight the Obsidian Order, to protect the universe, hinged on their ability to identify the

traitor before they struck again. The very act of self-
preservation demanded that they turn on each other, that
they question their loyalty, their motives, their very souls.

The investigation began slowly, painstakingly. They
reviewed every communication, every data transfer, every
interaction they'd had in the past few weeks. They
scrutinized each other's schedules, searching for
anomalies, inconsistencies, anything that might betray the
traitor's actions. The process was grueling, each discovery
deepening the chasm of suspicion between them.

Lena, fueled by a cold, relentless logic, focused on the
digital footprint. She meticulously examined the logs,
searching for unusual access patterns, unauthorized
downloads, any sign of data exfiltration. She found
anomalies, subtle deviations from the norm, small
alterations that indicated unauthorized access. But pinning
down the culprit required more than just technical
analysis; it demanded a deep understanding of human
behavior, of motivations and weaknesses.

Thorne, ever the intuitive scientist, took a more
psychological approach. He analyzed each member's
behavior, looking for signs of stress, guilt, or deception. He
noted the subtle shifts in body language, the fleeting
expressions, the almost imperceptible hesitations in
speech. He delved into their backgrounds, searching for

past conflicts, hidden agendas, anything that might explain their possible betrayal.

Hanson, meanwhile, found himself consumed by a spiral of self-doubt. The weight of suspicion pressed down on him, his own integrity feeling fragile and vulnerable. He had always prided himself on his loyalty, his unwavering commitment to the cause. Yet, the evidence against one of them – whether it was Lena, Thorne, or himself - seemed inescapable.

Days bled into weeks, the tension in the lab growing unbearable. The holographic galaxy, once a source of awe and wonder, now served as a constant reminder of the imminent danger they faced. The pressure mounted, pushing them to the brink of their sanity. The betrayer, lurking in plain sight, was chipping away at their collective spirit, making them question everything.

Then, a breakthrough. Lena discovered a hidden encrypted file, a small anomaly she'd almost overlooked. It was a backdoor, a clandestine communication channel used to secretly transmit data to an unknown recipient. The channel had been carefully disguised, masked within the legitimate traffic, but Lena's meticulous analysis had unearthed it. The data itself was encrypted, but the metadata, the digital fingerprints of the transmission, provided a critical clue.

The metadata pointed to a specific time and location, a moment when only one of them had been in close proximity to the server. Thorne, during a brief respite from his analysis, had allegedly accessed a rarely used diagnostic tool. He'd claimed it was necessary for a routine check, but the timing coincided perfectly with the illicit data transfer. The evidence, though circumstantial, was compelling.

The confrontation was swift and brutal. Thorne's demeanor shifted from weary exhaustion to a calculated calm. He admitted to his actions but vehemently denied being a traitor. He revealed that he'd been working on a contingency plan, a secret channel of communication designed to reach out to an independent organization dedicated to counter-acting the Obsidian Order. He explained he had intentionally obscured his actions due to mistrust and paranoia.

He had suspected a mole within the team and that this contingency was a way of circumventing any potential betrayal. His actions, though seemingly suspicious, were intended to protect their collective mission, not undermine it. The independent organization he'd contacted were experts in cybersecurity, and he'd shared some encrypted data with them hoping they could identify the true traitor within their ranks.

Lena, initially skeptical, eventually accepted Thorne's explanation. The data he had transmitted did not contain any strategic details about their mission or the counter-measure. She understood his intentions, even if his method had been reckless and potentially damaging.

But the relief was short-lived. While the immediate crisis had been averted, a deeper, more insidious betrayal still lurked in the shadows. The Obsidian Order was not merely interested in controlling dark energy; they were seeking something more, something far more sinister. The implications of the true betrayal, still hidden in the labyrinthine corridors of the universe, threatened to unravel everything they had worked for, to undo their every hard-won victory. The game was far from over; it had only just begun.

The Obsidian Orders Base

The biting Antarctic wind howled a mournful dirge around the makeshift camp, the icy breath stinging exposed skin. Dr. Aris Thorne shivered, pulling his thermal gear tighter, his breath misting in the frigid air. Beside him, Dr. Lena Hanson, her face etched with a mixture of determination and apprehension, stared at the coordinates displayed on her ruggedized tablet. They had been chasing shadows for weeks, following the cryptic clues embedded within the ancient book, a trail that had led them to this desolate, windswept corner of the world.

The coordinates, gleaned from a particularly challenging section of the text—a sequence of seemingly random numbers that had taken them days to decipher—indicated the location of the Obsidian Order's hidden base. It wasn't a geographical location in the traditional sense; it wasn't marked on any map, not even the most detailed satellite imagery. Instead, it was a location within a location, a hidden facility concealed beneath the seemingly impenetrable ice sheet.

"Are you sure about this, Aris?" Hanson asked, her voice barely audible above the wind's roar. "This feels... too easy. The Obsidian Order isn't known for leaving gaping holes in their security."

Thorne, his gaze fixed on the swirling snow, nodded grimly. "The book implied a level of sophistication far beyond our current understanding. Perhaps they've developed technology that allows them to shift their location, to become... undetectable." He paused, running a hand through his wind-tossed hair. "Or maybe they're simply overconfident."

Their journey to this point had been fraught with peril. They'd evaded the Order's relentless pursuit on several occasions, narrowly escaping ambushes that employed technology they could barely comprehend. The Order's operatives seemed to anticipate their every move, their actions suggesting a network of informants embedded within the scientific community, a network far-reaching and insidious.

Using a combination of satellite data and the book's increasingly deciphered clues, they had managed to pinpoint a subtle anomaly in the ice's thermal profile. A localized area of unusually high heat, buried deep beneath the surface, indicated a massive underground complex. It was a faint signal, easily missed, but it was there—a telltale sign of the Obsidian Order's technological hubris.

Hanson activated a compact, yet powerful, sonic emitter. The device, a prototype developed from her own research into high-frequency sound waves, was designed to penetrate the ice and create a temporary cavity, creating a pathway into the Obsidian Order's hidden world. The device hummed, emitting a high-pitched whine that was barely perceptible amidst the wind.

As the sonic waves pulsed, a section of the ice began to crack and fissure, revealing a yawning chasm that seemed to swallow the light. The air around them crackled with an unnatural energy, a palpable hum that vibrated through their very bones. The scent of ozone, sharp and metallic, filled the air.

They descended into the abyss using specialized equipment designed to withstand the extreme pressure and cold. The descent was slow and agonizing, each meter a testament to their courage and the urgency of their mission. As they approached the base, the temperature began to rise dramatically, a stark contrast to the icy world above.

The base itself was a marvel of engineering, a testament to the Order's technological prowess. It was a sprawling complex carved directly into the ice, its walls lined with glowing panels that emitted a soft, pulsating light. The air was thick with the hum of machinery, the constant thrum of advanced technologies operating at peak performance. It was a stark reminder of the technological chasm that separated them from their adversaries.

The complex was a labyrinthine structure, a series of interconnected tunnels and chambers that stretched as far as the eye could see. The walls pulsed with an otherworldly light, and the air hummed with the power of dark energy. They moved cautiously through the corridors, their footsteps echoing eerily in the vast, subterranean space.

They witnessed scenes that defied belief: vast chambers filled with strange machinery that hummed with dark energy, manipulating dark matter in ways that seemed impossible. They saw containment cells holding what appeared to be captured entities—creatures of pure dark matter, their forms shifting and swirling with an unsettling intelligence. It was a nightmarish vision of power beyond comprehension, a testament to the Obsidian Order's ambition and the profound dangers they posed.

The deeper they ventured, the more evident it became that the Obsidian Order wasn't merely researching dark matter and dark energy; they were weaponizing them. They were constructing devices capable of harnessing the power of these cosmic forces, devices capable of unimaginable destruction. The very fabric of reality seemed to warp and bend around these machines, a testament to the raw, untamed power they contained.

They discovered laboratories where scientists, their faces pale and drawn, worked tirelessly, their eyes filled with a mixture of fear and fanaticism. These scientists, once esteemed members of the scientific community, had been seduced by the Obsidian Order's promises of power and knowledge, blind to the potential consequences of their actions.

The deeper they went; the more uneasy Thorne and Hanson became. The air grew heavy, charged with an almost tangible sense of dread. They sensed they were being watched, their every move scrutinized by unseen eyes. The technology of the base was far beyond anything they'd ever encountered— a level of sophistication that suggested an alliance with an extraterrestrial intelligence, a knowledge that had been passed down through millennia.

They knew their mission was incredibly dangerous. They were facing an enemy with vastly superior resources and technological prowess, an enemy who possessed the power to reshape the universe itself. But they pressed on, driven by a desperate hope, a belief that they could still prevent the Obsidian Order from unleashing its devastating weapon upon the cosmos. Their journey had taken them to the heart of darkness, a place where the line between science and nightmare blurred. The confrontation was inevitable, a clash of wills, of science and fanaticism, where the fate of the universe itself hung precariously in the balance. And they knew, with chilling certainty, that there was no turning back.

Technological Superiority

The wind, a razor-edged sculptor, had carved the Antarctic ice into grotesque shapes, mirroring the twisted reality Aris and Lena now faced. Their makeshift camp, a pathetic defiance against the overwhelming hostility of the landscape, felt miles away from the theoretical equations and controlled environments of their usual work. The coordinates had led them to a chasm, a jagged wound in the earth's icy crust, its depths swallowed by an unnatural darkness that seemed to suck the light from the very air. This was where the Obsidian Order waited.

A low hum, almost imperceptible at first, began to resonate through the ice. It vibrated in their bones, a primal tremor that spoke of immense power. Lena gripped her tablet, her knuckles white. "They're here," she whispered, her voice barely audible above the wind's shriek.

From the chasm's depths, a light began to rise, not the warm glow of a star, but a cold, malevolent luminescence that painted the ice in shades of violet and deep indigo. It pulsed with an unsettling rhythm, mirroring the hum that was now a deafening roar. Slowly, a vessel emerged, defying gravity and terrestrial logic. It was sleek, obsidian black, and shaped like a teardrop, its surface shimmering with an ethereal energy. No visible engines or propulsion systems were apparent; it moved with an unnerving grace, as if guided by a force beyond human comprehension.

"Dark energy propulsion," Aris breathed, his voice laced

with awe and dread. "They've harnessed it... mastered it." The Obsidian Order's technological superiority was terrifyingly evident. Their understanding of dark energy, a force that constituted 68% of the universe's energy density, was far beyond anything Aris and Lena, or indeed the scientific community at large, had ever imagined. The Order's mastery wasn't just theoretical; it was practical, tangible, terrifyingly real. Their ship, a testament to this mastery, was a weapon in itself – capable, Aris suspected, of warping spacetime itself.

As the vessel settled silently on the ice, a ramp extended, its surface smooth as polished onyx. From the ship emerged figures cloaked in dark, flowing robes, their faces obscured by deep hoods. They moved with an unnerving stillness, an almost robotic precision, their presence exuding an aura of cold authority.

"They're not just manipulating dark energy," Lena pointed out, her gaze fixed on a faint shimmer emanating from the

figures' robes. "There's something else... dark matter."

Dark matter, the enigmatic substance that constituted approximately 85% of the universe's matter, was even more mysterious than dark energy. Its very nature was unknown; it interacted with ordinary matter only through gravity, leaving scientists baffled for decades. Yet, the Obsidian Order seemed to have not just detected but manipulated it. This was beyond comprehension. It implied a level of technological advancement so far beyond humanity's own that it bordered on the miraculous, or perhaps, the demonic.

The leader of the Obsidian Order stepped forward. His face, when he finally revealed it, was as gaunt and severe as the Antarctic landscape, his eyes burning with an unsettling intensity. He spoke in a low, resonant voice that seemed to echo the hum of the ship. "Dr. Thorne, Dr. Hanson. We have been expecting you."

Aris stepped forward, his own apprehension masked by a forced calm. "We know what you're doing. You're planning to weaponize dark energy and dark matter."

The leader gave a chilling laugh, a sound devoid of humor. "Weaponize? No, my dear doctor. We are not merely weaponizing it; we are harnessing its true potential. We are shaping the universe to our will."

He gestured towards the chasm. "Beneath this ice lies the nexus, a point of singularity where the barriers between dimensions are thin. We've established a stable wormhole, a gateway to unimaginable power. With this technology, we can rewrite the very fabric of reality. We can cleanse this

universe of its impurities, its weaknesses... its humanity."

Lena's breath hitched. The implications were staggering. The Obsidian Order wasn't merely after domination; they sought to reshape the universe, to eliminate what they considered imperfections. Humanity, in their eyes, was a flaw to be eradicated.

"You're mad," Aris stated, his voice tight. "This is cosmic hubris."

"Mad?" The leader's eyes blazed. "We are enlightened. We see the potential, the power that lies dormant within the universe. You, however, cling to your primitive understanding, blinded by your short-sighted morality." He paused, his gaze sweeping over Aris and Lena with a chilling assessment. "Your science is but a child's toy compared to our mastery."

The demonstration of their technological superiority was swift and brutal. The Obsidian Order deployed smaller vessels, similar to the mothership but smaller and nimbler, each one humming with the same unnerving energy. These craft moved with impossible speed and precision, their movements defying the laws of physics as they manipulated gravitational fields with seeming ease. They could teleport, phasing through solid matter as if it were air, reappearing in a new location with frightening speed and silent efficiency.

Aris watched, his mind racing, trying to understand the physics behind these displays. The energy signatures suggested a manipulation of quantum entanglement on an unimaginable scale, a technology that could instantaneously transmit information or even matter across vast distances. It wasn't just speed; it was a fundamental rewriting of spatial limitations. The implications for warfare were devastating.

Lena, equally horrified, examined the data streaming into her tablet. "They're using dark matter as a shield," she said, her voice strained. "It bends light and even energy, rendering

conventional weapons useless. It's almost... invisible."

The Order's technological advantage wasn't just in weaponry; it was in defense. Their ability to manipulate dark matter made them virtually invulnerable to attack. Their shields weren't simply energy barriers; they were distortions of spacetime itself, rendering even the most advanced weaponry ineffective. This realization sent a chill down Aris's spine. They were outmatched, outgunned, outclassed in every conceivable way.

Aris and Lena's hope, fragile as it already was, seemed to crumble. Facing an enemy with such a staggering technological lead, a lead that stemmed from a mastery of forces humanity barely understood, felt utterly hopeless. The universe's fate, it seemed, rested on a precipice, balanced on the razor's edge of their adversary's terrifying technological prowess. The confrontation had begun, and the odds were overwhelmingly against them. The fight for survival, for the very existence of humanity, had begun in earnest, in the heart of the Antarctic wilderness, against a power that seemed capable of reshaping the very fabric of reality.

A Desperate Plan

The biting Antarctic wind howled a mournful dirge around their makeshift camp, a stark counterpoint to the frantic calculations scribbled across Aris's notepad. Lena, her face etched with exhaustion and grim determination, monitored the readings from their salvaged satellite uplink. The Obsidian Order's presence loomed, a palpable threat that hung heavier than the oppressive ice above them. Their initial confrontation had been a brutal wake-up call— a stark demonstration of the Order's technological supremacy. They were facing an enemy who seemed to bend the laws of physics to their will, an enemy armed with weaponry far beyond human comprehension. Hope felt like a luxury they could no longer afford.

"The energy readings are spiking again," Lena announced, her voice tight with apprehension. "Their activity is

intensifying. They're... preparing something."

Aris, his eyes bloodshot from lack of sleep, barely glanced up. He was lost in a maelstrom of equations, a desperate attempt to decipher the cryptic symbols gleaned from the ancient book—the very book that had brought them to this desolate, life-threatening place. The book held the key, he believed, the key to understanding the Order's power, and perhaps, to countering it.

"Thorne and Hanson's data... it's the only chance we have," Aris muttered, his gaze finally leaving the intricate calculations. He referred to the two theoretical physicists, now deceased, whose research had provided the foundation for their understanding of the Order's technology. Their work, though incomplete and fragmented, hinted at a vulnerability in the Order's seemingly impenetrable defenses.

Lena nodded, understanding dawning in her eyes. "The resonance cascades. Disrupt their energy field by exploiting the harmonic instability in their power source. It's a long shot, but..." She trailed off, the unspoken implications hanging heavy in the frigid air. The plan was audacious, bordering on suicidal.

Thorne and Hanson's theory proposed that the Order harnessed a previously unknown cosmic force, manipulating it through a sophisticated network of interconnected resonators. These resonators, scattered across the globe, amplified the cosmic energy, creating a powerful, weaponized field. The theory further suggested that the network was inherently unstable, vulnerable to a carefully calculated disruption – a resonance cascade that could overload the system, causing a catastrophic failure.

The risk was immense. A miscalculation, even a minor one, could lead to an unpredictable chain reaction, potentially unleashing a devastating energy surge that would engulf the entire planet. The success rate was minuscule, barely more than a whisper of hope in the face of certain annihilation.

But it was their only hope.

"We need to pinpoint the primary resonator," Aris said, his voice firm despite the tremor in his hands. "The book... it holds clues. The geometric patterns... they're not random.

They're a map."

For days, they worked tirelessly, deciphering the ancient text, its alien symbols slowly yielding their secrets. The patterns revealed a complex network of energy conduits, pulsating veins of cosmic power that spanned the globe. The primary resonator, the heart of the Order's system, was located not in some high-tech facility, but in an unexpected place: the submerged ruins of an ancient civilization, hidden deep beneath the Pacific Ocean.

"The irony," Lena murmured, tracing a finger along a particularly intricate sequence of symbols. "They harnessed the power of the cosmos, yet they're rooted in the past. In our past."

The plan was a multi-stage operation, demanding precision and timing. First, they needed to reach the underwater ruins. This required securing a deep-sea submersible—a task almost as daunting as their central objective itself. They needed to infiltrate the ruins undetected, bypass the Order's advanced security systems, and then, using a device they had painstakingly constructed based on Thorne and Hanson's fragmented research, trigger the resonance cascade.

The device was a delicate instrument, a finely tuned symphony of advanced electronics and exotic materials. It resembled a bizarrely shaped tuning fork, its prongs etched with intricate circuitry. It was designed to emit a specific frequency, a harmonic counterpoint to the Order's energy field, thus creating the cascade. The slightest deviation could result in catastrophic failure, leading to devastating consequences.

Their journey to the underwater ruins was fraught with peril. They were pursued by the Order's advanced aerial drones, their movements tracked and intercepted by unseen forces. They evaded capture by a hair's breadth, relying on their wits and a combination of luck and cunning to outmaneuver their relentless pursuers. The submersible, salvaged from a derelict research facility, creaked and groaned under the immense pressure of the deep ocean, a constant reminder of their precarious situation.

The ruins, when they finally reached them, were a breathtaking and terrifying spectacle. Ancient stone structures, covered in strange symbols similar to those in the book, rose from the seabed like ghostly monuments to a forgotten civilization. These were not merely ruins, but the remnants of a once-great civilization that had somehow mastered the very forces the Obsidian Order now sought to weaponize.

Inside the primary resonator chamber, the air hung heavy with the thrumming energy of the cosmic force. The chamber itself resembled a colossal engine, humming with almost palpable power. Aris and Lena carefully positioned their device, the delicate instrument vibrating slightly in their hands. It was now or never.

"Ready?" Aris asked, his voice barely a whisper.

Lena nodded, her eyes fixed on the pulsating energy field.

"Let's end this."

With a shared glance, they activated the device. A high-pitched whine filled the chamber, a sound that seemed to tear at the very fabric of reality. The energy field around them intensified, radiating a blinding light. The resonance cascade had begun. The entire chamber began to vibrate with increasing intensity. The ground beneath their feet shook violently. The walls crackled with energy, threatening to collapse.

The results were immediate, yet utterly unpredictable. The cascade caused a ripple effect across the planet. The Order's technological systems failed, their weapons deactivated. A wave of energy pulsed out from the resonator, causing disruptions across the planet. But it wasn't destruction, as the earlier theory had partially suggested. It was something more... a reset. A cleansing.

The ancient technology that powered the Order simply... ceased to function, its power drained. The Obsidian Order, once an unstoppable force, was suddenly vulnerable, their dominion over the cosmic energy shattered. The risk they'd taken, a leap of faith into the unknown, had paid off. But the universe held countless other secrets, and Aris and Lena knew, as the tremors subsided and the light dimmed, their journey had just begun. The fight was far from over. They had merely won a battle in a war of cosmic proportions.

The First Assault

The crimson sun dipped below the jagged peaks of the alien landscape, casting long, skeletal shadows that danced with the dust devils swirling across the plains. Thorne, his face streaked with grime and sweat, watched the wreckage of the assault drones smolder. The air, thick with the metallic tang of burning circuitry and the acrid bite of ozone, stung his lungs. He'd lost half his squadron in the first wave. The Obsidian Order's defenses, far more sophisticated than their initial reconnaissance suggested, had shredded their meticulously planned attack like tissue paper.

Hanson, his usually sharp features etched with grim determination, approached, his boots crunching on the shattered remnants of their advanced weaponry. "We underestimated them, Thorne," he stated, his voice devoid of emotion. "Their energy shields are far more resilient than we anticipated, and their countermeasures... well, they're something out of a nightmare."

Thorne nodded, the weight of the losses heavy on his shoulders. He ran a hand through his sweat-matted hair, the gesture betraying his inner turmoil. Their initial strategy, a swift, decisive strike aimed at crippling the Order's central power core, had failed spectacularly. The Order's response had been swift and brutal, a coordinated barrage of energy blasts that had overwhelmed their shields. The drones, cutting-edge technology designed to withstand extreme conditions, were reduced to molten slag in seconds.

"We need a new approach," Thorne said, his gaze fixed on the distant, ominous silhouette of the Order's base, a monolithic structure that seemed to claw its way out of the very planet itself. "A frontal assault is suicidal."

Hanson, ever the pragmatist, agreed. "We need to exploit their weaknesses. Their energy shields, while potent, seem to have a recharge cycle. Our sensor data suggests a brief period of vulnerability between blasts."

"A window of opportunity, you mean," Thorne mused, leaning against a scorched drone chassis. The heat radiated from the metal, a tangible reminder of the battle's ferocity. "A tiny window, against an enemy that seems to anticipate our every move. And that's not even considering their other weapons. The graviton disruptors nearly ripped our lead

drone apart before it even reached the perimeter."

The graviton disruptors, Hanson recalled, were particularly terrifying. They could manipulate gravity fields on a localized scale, creating pockets of intense gravitational force that tore apart anything caught within their radius. It was a weapon that defied conventional warfare strategies.

"We need to strike at their logistics, their supply lines," Hanson suggested. "If we can disrupt their ability to replenish their resources, their defenses will weaken over time." He pointed toward a jagged canyon that snaked its way toward the base. "Their primary energy conduits run through that canyon. A targeted strike there might cripple their power grid."

Thorne considered the proposal. It was a far riskier strategy than a direct attack, but their previous failure had shown them the futility of brute force. "It's a long shot," he admitted. "The canyon is heavily guarded. We'll need a

stealth approach, and even then, we'll be outnumbered." "We'll use cloaking technology," Hanson replied, a flicker of grim determination in his eyes. "The new experimental cloaking devices, the ones from Project Nightingale? They're still experimental, but with the right configuration, they might just buy us the time we need."

The next few days were a blur of frantic activity. Thorne and Hanson oversaw the preparation of a smaller, more agile team, focusing on stealth and precision rather than sheer firepower. They re-tooled existing drones, equipping them with specialized EMP bursts designed to temporarily disable the Order's energy shields, creating that critical window of vulnerability Hanson had identified.

The cloaking devices, as Hanson had warned, were unstable. They pulsed and flickered, sometimes momentarily dropping their camouflage. It was a nerve-wracking experience, navigating the treacherous terrain of the alien landscape while constantly battling the limitations of the technology. The very air seemed to hum with tension, every rock and shadow seeming to conceal a hidden danger.

The operation was meticulously planned, each step carefully calculated, every possible contingency accounted for. The plan was audacious, bordering on reckless, but it was their only chance. Failure meant not just defeat but complete annihilation. They were fighting for more than just survival; they were fighting to prevent the Obsidian Order from unleashing their devastating power upon the rest of the galaxy.

The final approach was agonizingly slow. The cloaking devices worked intermittently, resulting in several near misses as patrol drones almost detected their presence. Thorne, tense and alert, guided his team through the shadowed canyon, his heart pounding in his chest like a war drum. Each flicker of the cloaking device was a jolt of adrenaline, reminding him how precarious their situation truly was.

They finally reached their target – a massive energy conduit pulsating with an ominous blue light. The conduit was heavily guarded, but the EMP bursts, precisely timed and targeted, managed to momentarily disable the energy shields of the guarding units, creating that precious window of opportunity.

The attack was swift and decisive. Specialized disruptors, smaller and more maneuverable than the earlier drones, struck at the energy conduit's core. The ensuing explosion was spectacular, a colossal burst of energy that lit up the night sky with a blinding flash. The ground trembled under the force of the blast.

Their mission accomplished, the team retreated, navigating the chaotic aftermath of the explosion and avoiding the enraged Order forces scrambling to contain the damage. The cloaking devices, already nearing their operational limits, finally gave out just as they reached the relative safety of the higher ground.

The return journey was even more perilous than the approach. The Order's forces were now on high alert, swarming the canyon like angry hornets. They used every ounce of their skill and ingenuity to evade pursuit, narrowly avoiding detection multiple times. The tension was almost unbearable, each moment a testament to their tenacity and skill.

They eventually reached their base, battered but alive. The success was bittersweet. They had struck a blow against the Obsidian Order, inflicting significant damage on their infrastructure. But the cost had been high. They had lost more drones, and the strain on their technology was immense. The war was far from over. The Obsidian Order, wounded but not defeated, would surely retaliate. The universe was vast and unpredictable, and the challenges ahead loomed large. But for now, they had bought themselves some time. A precious, hard-fought victory in a war that threatened the very fabric of existence. The battle was won, but the war... oh, the war had just begun.

Unexpected Allies

The flickering holographic display in the command center cast an eerie green glow on Thorne's weary face. The losses from the previous assault hung heavy in the air, a palpable silence broken only by the hum of the damaged power generators. He ran a hand through his already disheveled hair, the grime clinging stubbornly to his skin, a physical manifestation of the battle's toll. Their victory had been pyrrhic, a hard-won respite in a war that showed no signs of ending.

Suddenly, a sharp crackle pierced the silence. A new signal, unlike anything they'd encountered before, pulsed on the main console. It was a coded message, encrypted with an algorithm so complex that even their most advanced decryption programs struggled to unravel it. Dr. Aris Thorne, the team's resident cryptographer, her eyes magnified behind thick glasses, worked frantically, her fingers flying across the keyboard.

"It's...it's breaking," she breathed, her voice tight with a mix of excitement and apprehension. "An unknown language, but the underlying structure...it's consistent with a form of

quantum entanglement communication. Unheard of."

As the last piece of the code fell into place, a series of images appeared on the screen. They weren't still images; they were three-dimensional renderings, holographic projections of beings unlike anything Thorne had ever seen. Tall, slender figures with skin like polished obsidian and eyes that shimmered with an inner light. They were ethereal, almost spectral, yet undeniably real.

The accompanying message, now translated, sent a chill down Thorne's spine. It wasn't a declaration of war, or a threat. It was an offer of alliance. The beings, who identified themselves as the Luminians, had been monitoring the Obsidian Order's activities for centuries. They possessed technology far beyond anything humanity had ever conceived, and they were willing to share it – if Thorne and his team were willing to cooperate.

Thorne felt a wave of disbelief wash over him. An alliance with beings from another galaxy? It was too fantastical, too much like the science fiction novels he'd devoured as a child. Yet the evidence was irrefutable. The holographic projections were impossibly detailed, the translation flawless. The Luminians claimed to understand the Obsidian Order's ultimate goals, a chilling prophecy of universal annihilation that echoed Thorne's own deepest fears. They revealed that the Obsidian Order wasn't merely conquering planets; they were harvesting a unique form of dark energy, a force that could unravel the fabric of spacetime itself.

The risk was immense. Trusting the Luminians, a race they knew virtually nothing about, felt like a gamble with the very fate of existence. Their advanced technology was a double-edged sword; it could save them, or it could enslave them. But inaction was not an option. The Obsidian Order was closing in, their relentless advance pushing Thorne and his team to the brink of annihilation. The alliance presented itself as a desperate, last-ditch attempt to survive.

The Luminians' offer wasn't entirely altruistic. They were a dying race, their home world ravaged by a celestial event that had crippled their ability to sustain life. They needed humanity's resources, its resilience, to help them rebuild. In essence, the alliance was a mutual pact of survival. Humanity would receive advanced technology and tactical support; the Luminians would gain access to resources and a strategic foothold in a corner of the galaxy they could still save.

Thorne convened an emergency meeting. The tension in the room was thicker than the dust outside. His team, initially skeptical, were slowly won over by the weight of evidence and the gravity of the situation. The Luminians were offering a lifeline, but it was a treacherous rope bridge spanning a chasm of uncertainty.

The initial contact was tentative, fraught with suspicion and mistrust. The Luminians communicated through a combination of holographic projections and complex mathematical equations, their language far removed from human understanding. But as they worked together, coordinating strategies and sharing information, a grudging respect blossomed.

The Luminians' technology was breathtaking, far exceeding any human achievement. They introduced Thorne to weapons systems that could neutralize entire fleets with pinpoint accuracy, cloaking devices that rendered their ships invisible to the Obsidian Order's sensors, and energy sources that were practically limitless. The training was rigorous, pushing the human team to the absolute limit of their capabilities. But the Luminians' instructors, despite their alien physiology, possessed a surprising amount of patience and understanding.

As they delved deeper into their shared fight, unexpected similarities emerged between the two species. Both were driven by a profound need to protect their world, their people. Both valued knowledge and innovation, a shared commitment that went beyond their physical differences. The Luminians, despite their advanced civilization, possessed a spiritual understanding of the universe that deeply resonated with Thorne. Their connection to their home world, even in its ruined state, provided an unexpected sense of comfort.

The alliance, however, was not without its internal conflicts. Some of Thorne's team struggled to accept the Luminians, their inherent xenophobia and ingrained biases difficult to overcome. The cultural chasm was profound. But as they fought side-by-side against a common enemy, these divisions slowly began to fade. The shared experience of facing annihilation forged an unlikely bond, proving that survival often transcends even the deepest prejudices.

The next assault on the Obsidian Order's stronghold was vastly different. The Luminians' technology provided a decisive advantage. Their cloaking devices allowed them to bypass the enemy's defenses, their advanced weaponry decimating the enemy forces with surgical precision. The Obsidian Order, caught completely off guard, was forced into a desperate retreat. The victory was overwhelming, a resounding triumph that shifted the balance of power in the war.

But the alliance, forged in the crucible of conflict, remained precarious. The Luminians, despite their seeming altruism, had their own agenda. Thorne knew that their cooperation wasn't based solely on shared interests. There was an element of manipulation, a strategic calculation that played into their own survival. He couldn't quite decipher their true motives.

As the battle subsided, leaving behind a landscape littered with the remnants of the Obsidian Order's defeated forces, Thorne looked up at the shimmering stars. The war was far from over. The Obsidian Order would regroup, its resources depleted but its resolve still burning fiercely. But now, Thorne had unexpected allies, allies who possessed the power to tilt the scales of the cosmic conflict – if they could maintain trust, and if they could decipher the Luminians' true intentions. The universe, once again, felt both terrifying and strangely hopeful. The fight for survival had brought together two vastly different species, bound together not by choice, but by fate, their destinies intertwined in a cosmic dance of survival. The unexpected alliance had reshaped the battlefield, but the war for the universe's fate was far from won.

The Final Confrontation

The air crackled with a palpable tension, a silent scream echoing in the heart of the Obsidian Order's base. It wasn't the hum of machinery, though the facility throbbed with the energy of a thousand suns harnessed and controlled. No, this was something deeper, a discordant note in the symphony of the cosmos itself, a dissonance born from the manipulation of forces beyond human comprehension. Dr. Aris Thorne, his face grim, his eyes burning with a fierce determination, surveyed the scene. Around him, the chaotic battlefield was a testament to the brutal fight that had preceded this final stand. Shattered fragments of advanced technology littered the floor, glowing with an eerie, internal light – remnants of the Order's attempts to weaponize the very fabric of spacetime.

Lena Hanson, her breath ragged, stood beside him, her hand resting on the ancient book – the source of both their power and their peril. The book pulsed with a faint, ethereal glow, resonating with the chaotic energies of the base, a silent heartbeat in the center of the storm. They had come a long way, from the quiet observatory where the book was first discovered to this heart of technological darkness. Their journey had been a harrowing odyssey through the deepest mysteries of the universe, a chase across the cosmic tapestry woven with threads of dark matter and dark energy.

Before them, the Obsidian Order's forces stood arrayed, a formidable army of genetically enhanced soldiers and cybernetically augmented warriors. Their eyes glowed with an unnatural light, reflecting the dark energy that coursed through their veins, transforming them into living weapons. Leading them was a figure shrouded in shadow, his face hidden behind a sleek, obsidian mask – the enigmatic leader of the Order, known only as "The Overseer."

The Overseer raised a hand, and the air itself seemed to crackle with anticipation. "Your defiance ends here," his voice boomed, amplified by the base's sophisticated sound system, a cold, metallic tone echoing through the cavernous space. "The universe will bend to our will, whether you like it or not."

Thorne met the Overseer's gaze, his own eyes unwavering. "The universe is not yours to control," he retorted, his voice steady, defying the overwhelming power arrayed against

him. "It belongs to all of us."

The battle began with a terrifying intensity. Energy blasts ripped through the air, leaving trails of searing plasma in their wake. The Obsidian Order's soldiers advanced with ruthless efficiency, their movements honed to a lethal precision. Thorne and Hanson, however, were not unprepared. They had learned from their previous encounters, adapting their strategy to the formidable technological superiority of their foes.

Hanson, using the knowledge gleaned from the ancient book, manipulated the ambient dark energy, weaving it into shields that deflected the Order's attacks. The book, a conduit of cosmic power, responded to her touch, pulsating with an otherworldly energy. Meanwhile, Thorne, utilizing his deep understanding of astrophysics, exploited the base's own energy grid, redirecting power flows and causing short circuits that disrupted the Order's weaponry.

The fight was a desperate dance between brilliant science and terrifying power. Each parry, each riposte, was a gamble played with the fate of the universe as the stakes. As the battle raged, the ancient book revealed more of its secrets, unveiling previously incomprehensible passages that unlocked unforeseen abilities. Hanson discovered how to channel the book's power, focusing the ambient dark energy into concentrated bursts that could disable enemy weapons and even overwhelm the Order's cybernetic enhancements.

But the Obsidian Order's resources were vast. They unleashed a wave of heavily armed drones, swarming Thorne and Hanson, their weapons a relentless barrage of energy and kinetic force. The drones were agile, their

movements unpredictable, their coordinated attacks
designed to overwhelm any defense.

The struggle was intense. Thorne, using his ingenuity,
managed to hack into the drone control system,
temporarily disrupting their attack. He and Hanson found
themselves fighting not only the Order's soldiers but also a
relentless tide of robotic enemies, each one a miniature
weapon of mass destruction. Every moment felt like
eternity, a blur of motion, of light, of intense struggle.

In the midst of the chaos, a devastating attack crippled
their defenses. A concentrated beam of dark energy, fired
from one of the Overseer's personal weapons, pierced their
shields, sending tremors through the base. Hanson was
thrown back, hitting a wall with a sickening thud. Thorne
knew they couldn't sustain this kind of assault; the
Obsidian Order's relentless attacks were slowly
overwhelming them.

As Thorne fought to protect Hanson, he realized the book's
power was depleting, the glow fading, the pulses
weakening. It seemed the battle was truly coming down to
their wits and courage.

He saw an opening, a weakness in the Order's defenses, a
small window of opportunity that might be their only
chance at victory. A risky maneuver, one that demanded

incredible precision and a complete gamble. But they had no other choice. With the last vestiges of the book's power, he amplified a wave of dark energy, a concentrated blast precisely aimed at the core power source of the Obsidian Order's base, a hidden chamber where the dark energy was being harnessed and weaponized.

The resulting explosion was catastrophic. The base shook violently, the ground trembling beneath their feet. Walls collapsed, the air filled with dust and debris. The Overseer's mask shattered, revealing a face contorted in a silent scream of rage and defeat. The once-formidable Obsidian Order was now a disorganized rabble, their power source destroyed, their weapons rendered useless.

But victory came at a price. The book was spent, its power depleted, its pages now blank, devoid of the ancient knowledge that had saved them. Hanson, badly injured, lay unconscious in Thorne's arms. Thorne himself was exhausted, battered, but alive. They had won the battle, but the war was far from over. The universe had been saved, but the lingering threat of unforeseen consequences haunted the victory. They had seen the true face of cosmic power, its awesome potential and terrifying implications. And they knew their journey, a journey of discovery and desperation, was far from over. The universe had been saved, but the lingering questions and the potential for future threats remained unanswered and unresolved. Their

victory had merely ushered in a new era of uncertainty, a
new chapter in the unfolding saga of the cosmos.

The Power of the Book

The silence that followed the cessation of hostilities was
deafening. The air, thick with the lingering scent of ozone
and burnt metal, hung heavy in the cavernous Obsidian
Order base. Dr. Aris Thorne, his breath ragged, his body
screaming in protest, gently laid Hanson down on a
relatively intact section of floor. The young physicist's face
was pale, his breathing shallow, but the steady rhythm of
his pulse offered a fragile reassurance. Thorne knew he
needed medical attention, and soon, but there was
something else that demanded his immediate attention –
the Book.

The ancient tome, its cover now scorched and cracked, lay
open on a nearby console, its pages remarkably unscathed
despite the cataclysmic events surrounding it. The glyphs,
previously indecipherable, now pulsed with a faint, internal
luminescence, a silent testament to the immense power
they had unleashed. It was clear now; the book wasn't
merely a repository of knowledge; it was a conduit, a key to
manipulating the very fabric of spacetime itself. The battles

they had fought, the impossible feats they had achieved –
all had been powered by the book's cryptic wisdom.

Thorne traced a finger across a particularly intricate glyph,
feeling a faint tingle run up his arm. The glyph seemed to
resonate with his own energy, a subtle feedback loop
establishing a connection. He recalled the frantic moments
during the battle, the sheer desperation that had driven
him to experiment with the book's power, the chaotic
energy he'd channelled to disrupt the Order's spacetime
manipulation devices. It had been a gamble, a desperate
act of defiance against forces that seemed overwhelmingly
powerful. But the gamble had paid off.

As Thorne focused his attention, the glyphs began to shift
and rearrange themselves, forming new patterns, new
equations. He understood now, or at least, he thought he
did. The book didn't contain fixed knowledge; it was a
dynamic system, a living library that adapted to the user's
needs, revealing its secrets only to those who understood
its language – the language of the cosmos. He had seen
glimpses of it before, during the previous battles, but the
true extent of its capabilities only became evident in this
moment of quiet aftermath.

He noticed a specific sequence of symbols, repeating across
multiple pages. It seemed to represent a mathematical
equation, complex and elegant, far beyond anything he'd

ever encountered. But as he stared at it, it began to resolve itself in his mind, translating itself from arcane symbols into comprehensible physics. He saw the equations representing a hitherto unknown form of energy manipulation – a way to harness and control the dark energy that constituted the majority of the universe. It was a terrifying and exhilarating realization simultaneously.

This dark energy, usually considered a constant, an invisible force pushing the universe's expansion, was, the book revealed, not a constant at all. It was a dynamic, controllable force, capable of incredible feats, from manipulating gravity to warping spacetime. The Obsidian Order had sought to weaponize it, to harness its destructive potential. But Thorne, through the book, had learned to understand and control it, turning the Order's weapon against them. He had effectively used their own science against them.

The book also revealed other secrets, details about the universe's structure, hints of the existence of other dimensions, and the potential for interdimensional travel.

These were not just abstract concepts but tangible possibilities, pathways paved by the book's intricate knowledge. The implications were staggering. The entire fabric of their understanding of the universe would be irrevocably altered.

The understanding wasn't immediate, however. It was a gradual revelation, a process of interpretation, a conversation between the book and Thorne's mind. He spent hours painstakingly deciphering the remaining glyphs, each new understanding opening up further layers of complex information. The book was a puzzle box of immense complexity, constantly shifting and evolving, presenting him with new challenges and rewards. He was a student again, a humble apprentice seeking knowledge from a far more ancient and powerful master.

As dawn broke, casting long shadows across the devastated facility, Thorne felt a surge of understanding, a clarity of thought that defied his exhaustion. He had not just survived; he had learned, grown, evolved. The book had given him more than just power; it had given him knowledge, a deeper appreciation for the universe's intricate workings, and a profound sense of responsibility. The responsibility to protect this knowledge, to use it wisely, to ensure it never fell into the wrong hands again.

But the victory was bittersweet. Hanson remained unconscious. Thorne carefully checked his vitals, a silent prayer forming on his lips. The young physicist was critical, the injuries sustained in the battle too severe for Thorne's limited medical skills. He knew he needed help, outside help. He needed to reach civilization, to alert the authorities, to share his discoveries, before anyone else could exploit them.

He had to leave, but leaving the book felt like a betrayal. It felt like abandoning a powerful ally, a source of profound and dangerous knowledge. But leaving it behind was simply not an option. Its power, while incredible, was double-edged. The potential for misuse, for catastrophic consequences, was too great. He couldn't risk leaving it behind, not now.

He carefully closed the book, feeling its weight, its power, pressing against his fingertips. It felt warm, almost alive. As he prepared to leave, he felt a sudden surge of energy, a wave of power emanating from the book itself. It was as if the book was trying to communicate something to him, a final message before he left. The glyphs pulsed one last time, then settled, leaving him with a single, clear image imprinted in his mind – a constellation, a unique pattern of stars never before catalogued. It was a coordinate, a location, possibly a new home for this dangerous and powerful relic.

The image faded, but the urgency of its message remained. He knew he had to reach this location, to find a way to protect the book and its knowledge, to safeguard humanity from its potentially destructive power. This was just the beginning of a new, more dangerous chapter. The battle was won, but the war, the true cosmic war for the fate of the universe, had just begun. The secrets held within the book were far more profound, far more devastating, than anyone could have ever imagined, and he, Aris Thorne, now bore the burden of their protection. The weight of the universe rested upon his shoulders, a weight he knew he would carry with unwavering determination. His journey was far from over. The universe had more to reveal, and he was ready to unravel its mysteries, no matter the cost.

Sacrifices Made

The coordinates pulsed on the worn data pad, a sickly green glow against Thorne's grime-stained fingers. The Obsidian Order's base, now a smoldering ruin, offered little comfort. The air, still thick with the metallic tang of destruction, felt heavy on his lungs, mirroring the weight of his responsibility. Hanson, miraculously alive though grievously wounded, lay on a makeshift stretcher fashioned from salvaged metal plating. His shallow breaths rasped a counterpoint to the ominous silence.

Thorne knew the journey ahead would be perilous. The location the Book's fading image had revealed was a remote Keplerian system, light years away, situated near a highly unstable neutron star. The sheer distance, the treacherous conditions, and the unknown threats that lurked in the void all weighed heavily on him. He glanced at the data pad again, the coordinates flickering like a malevolent eye. The sacrifice had already begun.

Reaching the Keplerian system demanded a sacrifice of resources beyond what he initially envisioned. The damaged escape pod, battered and scarred from the battle, was hardly suitable for interstellar travel. Repairing it would require sacrificing precious time, time he didn't have. He'd had to cannibalize parts from other wrecked craft, leaving them vulnerable, a silent testament to the choices he'd made.

But the true sacrifice lay in the choice of personnel. He had a small, hand-picked team, each member a specialist in their respective fields. Among them was Dr. Lena Petrova, a brilliant xeno-linguist, crucial for deciphering the Book's cryptic language; Commander Eva Rostova, a seasoned pilot whose courage and skill were matched only by her unwavering loyalty; and Jax, a seasoned engineer whose ingenuity had already proven invaluable in the battle. Each of them had families, lives, dreams they had to leave behind, a silent sacrifice they made for the greater good.

He knew that a simple rescue mission wouldn't be enough. This would be a fight for survival against the elements, and against whatever forces guarded the book's final resting place. The neutron star's intense gravity, the lethal radiation, the unpredictable solar flares – they were all formidable foes, each capable of snuffing out their lives in an instant. These were known perils, but the unknown remained the greatest threat.

The escape pod shuddered as it pierced through the warped fabric of spacetime, hurtling towards the Keplerian system. The journey was a brutal test of endurance, a testament to the sacrifices made. Weeks turned into months under the oppressive confines of the claustrophobic vessel. Rationing was strict, and the psychological strain of isolation threatened to unravel the crew. They faced moments of despair, their resilience tested to its limits. They had only the faint hope of succeeding, the weight of the universe resting heavily on their shoulders.

The neutron star loomed before them, a malevolent eye burning through the void. Its gravity was a palpable presence, threatening to crush their small vessel. They were caught in its gravitational dance, a delicate waltz between survival and annihilation. Eva's piloting skills were pushed to the very brink, her commands crisp and decisive. Jax constantly monitored the ship's systems, his eyes bloodshot, his movements a blur of frantic efficiency.

Lena, pale and drawn, spent hours poring over the fragmented data, the cryptic symbols of the Book twisting into a vortex that seemed to consume her.

But it was not only the physical dangers that tested them. The psychological toll of the mission was as severe as the physical. The isolation, the constant threat of death, the weight of responsibility – it chipped away at their resolve, pushing them to the limits of human endurance. Thorne watched, his heart aching, as the lines of worry deepened on their faces, the glow of determination dulled by weariness and fear. Each of them had sacrificed their peace of mind, their normal lives, their certainties for this impossible mission.

As they approached their destination, the neutron star's gravitational pull intensified. The ship groaned under the strain, its metal protesting with a chorus of creaks and groans. The threat of being torn apart was a constant companion, a chilling reminder of the sacrifices made. Even the smallest error could mean the end, a sacrifice they couldn't afford to make.

Their destination, a small, desolate planet orbiting the neutron star, was a barren rock, scarred and cratered by countless cosmic bombardments. The landscape was a testament to the violent forces at play, a stark reflection of the sacrifices they had already endured. Landing was a perilous maneuver, a dance between the extreme gravity and the uneven terrain. Each bump, each jolt, was a sharp reminder of the fragility of their situation.

Their arrival, however, was not met with the quiet solitude they had anticipated. A silent, watchful presence permeated the atmosphere, a sense of foreboding that wrapped itself around them like a shroud. The air crackled with an unseen energy, a sign that their mission was far from over. The final sacrifice may yet lie ahead.

They set up a temporary base in a cavern formed by an ancient impact. The air was thick with the metallic scent of the planet, a strange, alien odor that hung heavy in the air. The silence was absolute, broken only by the rhythmic hum of their life support systems, a mechanical heartbeat that punctuated the stillness. The Book's coordinates were locked onto a specific location within the crater, a point deep beneath the planet's surface.

The next phase demanded a different kind of sacrifice. Accessing the Book required traversing a labyrinthine tunnel system, a treacherous descent into the planet's unknown depths. The tunnels were narrow, claustrophobic, and unstable. The constant threat of cave-ins, toxic gases, and unseen creatures loomed over them, adding to the ever-present threat of the neutron star's volatile environment.

And as they delved deeper, Thorne realized that the greatest sacrifice was yet to come. The Book wasn't merely guarded; it was protected by a powerful, ancient entity. An entity that would test their resolve, their faith, their very humanity. The journey to the heart of the planet was a pilgrimage into the darkness, a descent into the unknown, where the lines between sanity and madness blurred, where the sacrifices made began to seem infinitesimally small in comparison to what they were yet to confront. The weight of the universe rested on their shoulders, the fate of all creation hanging in the balance. Their final sacrifice, perhaps, would be the ultimate price to pay for the preservation of existence itself. The battle for the universe, the cosmic war, had entered its final, most terrifying phase.

Turning the Tides

The crimson sun dipped below the jagged peaks of Xylos, casting long, skeletal shadows that danced with the flickering flames of their makeshift camp. Hanson, his face pale and drawn, coughed, a rattling sound that echoed the tremor in Thorne's own heart. The battle, far from over, had reached a terrifying new stage. They had breached the Obsidian Order's inner sanctum, a place of unimaginable power, but at a terrible cost. The sacrifice of their comrades still burned in Thorne's memory, a searing brand on his soul.

He looked at the artifact, the ancient Book, resting on a slab of obsidian, its pages shimmering with an ethereal light. It pulsed with a faint, rhythmic beat, a cosmic heartbeat echoing the universe's own rhythm. It wasn't just a book; it was a conduit, a gateway to energies beyond human comprehension. The Order hadn't merely guarded it; they had tried to control it, to harness its power for their own nefarious ends. And in doing so, they had awakened something far older, far more powerful.

The entity they had encountered—a being of pure energy, a consciousness woven into the fabric of spacetime—was not entirely hostile. Its actions were driven by a primal instinct to protect the balance of the universe, an instinct that saw the Order's actions as a catastrophic threat. But its methods were ruthless, its power overwhelming. Thorne and Hanson had barely escaped with their lives, their victory a pyrrhic one.

The key, Thorne realized, lay not in brute force, but in understanding. The Book wasn't a weapon to be wielded; it was a key to unlock the universe's secrets, a tool to negotiate with the cosmic entity. The cryptic symbols etched upon its pages weren't just random markings; they were a language, a form of communication that resonated with the entity's own essence.

Hanson, despite his injuries, was invaluable. His expertise in ancient languages, honed over decades of research, was their only hope of deciphering the Book's secrets. He painstakingly translated the symbols, each word a revelation, each sentence a step closer to understanding the entity's motivations. The Book spoke of a cosmic equilibrium, a delicate balance between creation and destruction, order and chaos. The Order's attempts to manipulate this equilibrium had triggered a counter-reaction, a desperate attempt by the universe to restore balance.

The entity, they discovered, was not a malevolent god, but a guardian, a protector. Its power wasn't meant to be controlled, but to be understood and respected. The Order's hubris had shattered this understanding, unleashing a force that threatened to unravel the fabric of reality itself.

Days bled into nights as they worked, their minds straining to comprehend the intricate cosmology detailed in the Book. They learned of celestial events that predated the formation of galaxies, of forces that warped spacetime and bent the laws of physics. The universe, they discovered, was far stranger and more wondrous than they could ever have imagined.

The turning point came unexpectedly. Thorne, fueled by a desperate hope, realized that the entity's power wasn't entirely destructive. It could be channeled, redirected. The Book wasn't just a key; it was a conductor, capable of harnessing the entity's energy and using it to restore balance.

Using a combination of ancient knowledge and cutting-edge technology, Thorne devised a plan. It was audacious, bordering on suicidal, but it was their only chance. They needed to create a resonance, a harmonic convergence between the Book's energy and the entity's consciousness. It was a gamble, a cosmic roll of the dice, but the stakes were too high to hesitate.

The process was delicate, requiring precise calibrations and perfect timing. Hanson, his body wracked with pain, guided Thorne, his voice a strained whisper amidst the hum of energy crackling around them. The Book glowed with an intense light, its pages swirling with ethereal patterns. The air crackled with energy, a tangible force that pressed against them, threatening to overwhelm them.

Then, as if by magic, the energy shifted. The chaotic, destructive power began to coalesce, forming a beam of pure energy that shot towards the heart of the planet, towards the epicenter of the Obsidian Order's disruption. It wasn't a weapon, but a restorative force, a cosmic balm capable of healing the wounds inflicted upon the universe.

The effect was immediate. The tremors that had plagued the planet ceased. The skies, once ablaze with unnatural energy, cleared, revealing a breathtaking panorama of stars. The entity's power, no longer a threat, became a source of protection, a shield against future threats.

The battle wasn't won by force, but by understanding. They hadn't conquered the cosmic entity; they had forged an alliance, a pact built on mutual respect and a shared understanding of the universe's intricate balance. Thorne and Hanson had turned the tides of the cosmic war, not through weapons or bloodshed, but through knowledge, through the power of understanding the universe's deepest secrets.

The aftermath was quiet, a stark contrast to the chaos that had preceded it. The Obsidian Order was gone, their power extinguished, their ambitions reduced to dust. But the Book remained, a testament to the universe's mysteries, a key to unlocking untold wonders. Thorne and Hanson, battered but unbroken, stood on the precipice of a new era, an era defined not by conflict, but by cooperation, an era where humanity's understanding of the cosmos had reached a new, profound level. The universe, they realized, was not a place of endless conflict, but a place of delicate balance, a place where the greatest victories were not achieved through violence, but through wisdom and understanding.

The weight of the universe, which had pressed down on them for so long, now felt lighter, though still immense. The responsibility they carried was not lessened; it had simply shifted. They were no longer just survivors; they were guardians, custodians of a knowledge that could shape the fate of worlds.

The Book's pages held countless other secrets, waiting to be discovered. New challenges would undoubtedly arise, but Thorne and Hanson were ready. They had stared into the abyss of cosmic conflict and emerged victorious, not through brute force but through a profound understanding of the universe's intricate workings. Their journey had just begun, a journey that would lead them to further discoveries, further challenges, and further revelations about the universe's timeless mysteries. The vastness of space, once a terrifying enigma, now held a promise—a promise of understanding, of exploration, and of a future where humanity's place in the cosmos was defined not by fear, but by knowledge and respect.

The faint glow of Xylos's twin moons painted the landscape in silver and gold as Thorne and Hanson prepared to leave. The planet, once a battleground, now stood as a testament to their triumph, a reminder of the power of knowledge and understanding in the face of overwhelming odds. The scars of the battle remained, both physical and emotional, but so did a quiet sense of hope, a belief that humanity could find its place among the stars, not as conquerors, but as responsible stewards of a universe far grander and more wondrous than they had ever dared to imagine. The journey was far from over, yet they stood ready to face whatever the cosmos threw their way, armed with the knowledge found within the ancient Book and a newfound respect for the universe's delicate equilibrium. The cosmic battle had ended, but the exploration of the cosmos had only just begun. The Book, now safely in their possession, held the key to unlocking untold secrets, promising a future filled with both peril and wonder. The universe awaited, and they were ready to answer its call.

Victory's Cost

The silence that followed the final collapse of the Obsidian Order's energy shield was deafening. Not the quiet of peace, but the quiet of exhaustion, of profound loss etched onto the very landscape of Xylos. The crimson dust, once swirling with the fury of plasma blasts and the shriek of disintegrating warships, settled slowly, coating everything in a fine, rust-colored shroud. Thorne stood amidst the wreckage, the acrid smell of ozone and burnt metal stinging his nostrils. Around him lay the twisted remains of their own ships, a grim testament to the battle's ferocity.

He knelt beside Hanson, who lay propped against a jagged rock, his breathing shallow and ragged. The younger man's face, usually bright with intellectual curiosity, was pale and drawn, etched with the lines of unimaginable stress. A deep gash marred his arm, a grim reminder of the energy blast that had nearly claimed him. Thorne gently cleaned the wound with a medic-gel, the cool liquid a stark contrast to the burning heat of Xylos's atmosphere.

"We did it, Thorne," Hanson whispered, his voice barely audible above the mournful sigh of the wind. "We won."

The words felt hollow, even as Thorne knew their truth. The victory felt more like a pyrrhic one, a triumph bought with a price far too steep. The faces of their fallen comrades flashed before his eyes – Captain Eva Rostova, her unwavering courage a beacon amidst the chaos; Dr. Jian Li, whose brilliant mind had been instrumental in deciphering the Book's secrets; Sergeant Miller, whose unwavering loyalty and unwavering aim had saved them countless times. Each loss resonated within him, a deep, aching wound that would likely never fully heal.

The cost extended beyond the human toll. Xylos itself bore the scars of the conflict. The once vibrant landscape was now a wasteland of shattered rock and scorched earth. The planet's delicate ecosystem, already strained by the Obsidian Order's presence, lay in tatters, the future uncertain. Their victory had come at the expense of a world, a testament to the destructive potential of unchecked ambition and the terrifying power wielded by the Obsidian Order.

Thorne gazed upon the ruins of the Order's citadel, a colossal structure of obsidian that had dominated the Xylosian landscape. Now, it was little more than a pile of rubble, its formidable defenses reduced to dust by the combined might of their fleet and the ingenious tactical maneuvers devised by Dr. Li. The citadel, a symbol of the Order's tyrannical rule, was gone, but the echoes of its oppression lingered, a haunting reminder of the darkness they had faced and overcome.

The Book, its cover now slightly scorched but otherwise intact, rested securely within a reinforced container strapped to Thorne's chest. It felt heavy, not just in weight, but in the sheer responsibility it represented. The knowledge contained within it held the potential to reshape humanity's destiny, to unlock unimaginable technological advancements and unravel the deepest mysteries of the cosmos. But it also held the potential for unimaginable destruction, a power that could be wielded for good or ill, depending on the hands that held it.

The weight of their victory pressed heavily on Thorne's shoulders. It was a victory hard-won, purchased with sacrifice, with blood spilled on alien soil. The universe, they had learned, was a vast and unforgiving place, where even the smallest act could have far-reaching consequences. Their victory felt less like a triumph and more like a somber reminder of their own mortality, a stark acknowledgment of the delicate balance between creation and destruction.

Hanson stirred, his eyes fluttering open. "The readings... they're stabilizing," he rasped, his voice weak but clear. "The energy surge... it's receding." He looked around at the desolation, his gaze filled with a mixture of awe and apprehension. "We've changed... everything."

Thorne nodded, his throat constricted with emotion. He knew Hanson was right. They had not only defeated the Obsidian Order but had irrevocably altered the course of galactic history. The power they now possessed, the knowledge within the Book, held the potential to shape the future of countless civilizations, to usher in an era of unprecedented technological advancement, or to plunge the galaxy into chaos. The responsibility was immense, a burden that rested heavily on their shoulders.

The next few days were a blur of activity. The surviving members of their fleet worked tirelessly, salvaging what they could from the wreckage, tending to the wounded, and securing the Book. They established a temporary base within the ruins of the Obsidian Order's citadel, the irony not lost on Thorne. The place that once symbolized oppression now served as a testament to their hard-fought victory. As they surveyed the damage, they began to grasp the scale of their achievement, and the weight of the responsibility they now carried.

The analysis of the battle's impact was a complex undertaking. The Obsidian Order's defeat had created a power vacuum, and other factions within the galaxy were poised to fill it. The knowledge contained within the Book, if exploited improperly, could empower these rival groups, potentially leading to even greater conflict. The delicate equilibrium they had painstakingly restored, was once again threatened. The battle for the galaxy, they now realized, was far from over. Their victory on Xylos was just a single, hard-won battle in a much larger, ongoing war.

They spent weeks studying the Book, poring over its cryptic passages and deciphering its ancient symbols. The knowledge contained within was astounding, exceeding their wildest expectations. It detailed the origins of the universe, the nature of dark matter and dark energy, and the existence of technologies far beyond their current comprehension. The book also described the rise and fall of numerous ancient civilizations, each leaving their own indelible mark on the cosmos. But amidst the wealth of knowledge, Thorne and Hanson discovered a disturbing truth: the Obsidian Order had not been the only force seeking to control the Book's power. They had been merely one piece in a much larger, more insidious game, a game played by entities far older and far more powerful than they could have imagined.

The implications were staggering. Their victory, though momentous, had only scratched the surface of a much larger conspiracy, a cosmic game of power and manipulation that had been unfolding for eons. The knowledge they possessed was both a blessing and a curse, a weapon that could be used to protect the galaxy or to destroy it. The choice, it seemed, rested solely with them.

The journey back to Earth was a silent one. The weight of
their victory, the profound loss they had suffered, and the
daunting challenges that lay ahead filled their thoughts.
The galaxy was a vast and unpredictable place, a realm of
both wonder and terror. They had glimpsed its immense
power, its capacity for both creation and destruction. They
had tasted victory, but at a steep cost, leaving them
changed, forever scarred by the battle on Xylos, forever
bound by the knowledge they now possessed. The universe
awaited, and they were ready to answer its call, armed with
the knowledge found within the ancient Book, and a
newfound respect for the universe's delicate and
unforgiving equilibrium. But the exploration of the cosmos
had only just begun; the true journey, the one fraught with
perilous challenges and unpredictable discoveries, lay
ahead.

The Universe Restored

The immediate aftermath was a silence so profound it felt heavier than the weight of a collapsing star. The chaotic energy surges that had wracked the Obsidian Order's base, the frantic bursts of dark matter manipulation, the desperate struggle for control over the very fabric of spacetime – it all ceased. A stillness descended, broken only by the rhythmic hiss of escaping gases and the occasional groan of twisted metal. The air, thick with the lingering scent of ozone and burnt circuitry, held a strange quietude, a stark contrast to the maelstrom that had preceded it.

Dr. Aris Thorne, his body bruised and aching, leaned against a shattered console, the ancient book clutched tightly in his hand. Its surface, once shimmering with an ethereal light, was now dull, almost lifeless. He felt the exhaustion gnawing at him, a profound weariness that settled deep in his bones. Lena Hanson, her face pale but resolute, knelt beside him, checking his pulse. The victory, hard-won and bought at a terrible price, felt less like triumph and more like a hollow echo.

The restoration of the universe wasn't a sudden, dramatic event. It wasn't a burst of light or a celestial chorus. Instead, it was a gradual unwinding, a subtle shift in the cosmic tapestry. The erratic fluctuations in the expansion rate, the unsettling distortions in spacetime – they began to smooth out, returning to a semblance of normalcy. The dark energy, no longer being manipulated and weaponized, started to resume its natural role in the universe's expansion, but not without leaving its mark.

The long-term consequences of the Obsidian Order's tampering were subtle yet pervasive. Astronomical observations in the following months revealed unusual gravitational anomalies in certain regions of space. These weren't the predictable, well-understood gravitational effects of stars and galaxies; these were strange, localized distortions, like ripples in a pond long after the stone has sunk. Scientists theorized that these were residual effects of the Order's experiments, lingering echoes of the manipulated dark matter and dark energy. Some regions showed an accelerated expansion, while others exhibited a slowing, a strange imbalance that threatened to create new pockets of instability within the cosmic fabric. The universe was healing, but the scars remained.

The legacy of the book itself was perhaps even more enigmatic. While much of its knowledge had been decoded and used to counter the Obsidian Order, vast portions remained stubbornly encrypted. The deciphered sections had provided invaluable insights into the nature of dark matter and dark energy – revealing them to be far more complex and sophisticated than previously imagined. They weren't just passive components of the universe; they held a kind of sentience, a rudimentary consciousness that interacted with the cosmos in ways humanity had only begun to comprehend. The remaining sections hinted at even greater complexities, suggesting that dark matter and dark energy were merely two components of a vast, interconnected cosmic intelligence that far surpassed human understanding. The book had offered a glimpse into this intelligence, but only a glimpse.

The implications were staggering. The universe itself, far from being a cold, indifferent void, seemed to possess a level of intelligence that was both awe-inspiring and deeply unsettling. It raised profound philosophical and theological questions about the nature of existence, humanity's place in the grand scheme of things, and the very definition of life itself. The book suggested that the universe had a history far older and richer than previously believed, a history populated by civilizations that had mastered the manipulation of cosmic forces, leaving behind only faint traces of their existence in the form of encrypted knowledge and subtle gravitational anomalies.

The fate of the Obsidian Order was a matter of debate. The base itself had been obliterated, their advanced technology destroyed. But the question of whether they had completely vanished remained open. There were persistent rumors of surviving cells, scattered operatives attempting to reconstruct their knowledge and capabilities. Some believed that the Order's influence had been completely eradicated, their ambition snuffed out before it could truly unfold. Others feared that the seeds of their dark ambition had been sown deep within the cosmic fabric, waiting for the right moment to sprout anew.

The aftermath also brought a profound reassessment of humanity's position in the cosmos. The near-extinction event had served as a stark reminder of humanity's vulnerability, its relative insignificance in the face of forces beyond its comprehension. Yet, it also brought a surge of unity and collaboration. The shared experience of facing annihilation had forged a new sense of global cooperation, a recognition that humanity's survival depended on shared knowledge and coordinated action. Space exploration programs received unprecedented funding and support. International collaborations on cosmic research intensified, with a shared focus on understanding the nature of dark matter, dark energy, and the universe's intricate, interwoven systems.

The long night of fear and uncertainty gave way to a tentative dawn. The universe, restored to a fragile balance, offered humanity a second chance, a chance to learn from its past mistakes and chart a new course toward a future built on understanding and respect for the cosmic forces that shaped its existence. The threat remained, lurking unseen in the shadows of the cosmos, but humanity, scarred but not broken, prepared to face it, armed with a newfound humility and a deeper understanding of the universe's awesome power.

The restoration was incomplete, the scars of the cosmic battle visible even in the tranquility that followed. The universe remained a mystery, a puzzle with countless pieces yet to be discovered. The ancient book, a silent testament to a forgotten civilization, still held secrets waiting to be unlocked, hinting at yet more perilous adventures, further explorations into the unknown depths of the cosmos. The new dawn was tinged with uncertainty, but it was a dawn nonetheless, a dawn that promised both immense peril and unimaginable wonder. The universe, restored, but forever changed, was waiting to be explored.

The Legacy of the Book

The acrid smell of ozone still clung to the air, a phantom reminder of the near-catastrophic event. Dust motes, illuminated by the weak, fractured light filtering through the debris-strewn sky, danced in the eerie silence. The Obsidian Order's base, once a bastion of forbidden knowledge and dark power, was now a ruin, a testament to the chaotic battle that had raged within its walls. But amidst the devastation, a sense of...resolution hung heavy in the air. The immediate threat, at least, was neutralized.

Dr. Aris Thorne, his face streaked with grime and exhaustion, knelt beside the shattered remains of the central console. His fingers, trembling slightly, traced the fractured surface of a crystalline structure, a fragment of the alien technology that had fueled the Order's manipulations of spacetime. The intricate carvings on the fragment, barely visible under the dust, resembled the glyphs from the ancient book – the very book that had precipitated this entire crisis. The book, currently secured in a Faraday cage within a heavily guarded bunker far removed from this ravaged landscape, remained the key. Its remaining, uninterpreted passages held the potential to both explain and perhaps even undo the lingering distortions in the fabric of spacetime.

The initial analysis of the recovered data from the console was both unsettling and awe-inspiring. The Obsidian Order hadn't merely been manipulating dark matter; they were attempting to harness a force far more fundamental, a force that seemed to precede the Big Bang itself. The data hinted at a level of cosmic engineering that dwarfed human comprehension. They spoke of manipulating the very constants of the universe, fine-tuning the strength of gravity, the speed of light, even the fundamental forces that govern reality. The audacity of their plan was breathtaking, a testament to their ambition and their profound misunderstanding of the forces they were attempting to control. Their hubris, however, had been their undoing. The universe, it seemed, had a way of resisting such audacious attempts at manipulation.

The team, assembled from the remnants of various scientific and governmental organizations, worked tirelessly, analyzing the salvaged data, deciphering the cryptic inscriptions within the book, and attempting to comprehend the sheer scale of the Obsidian Order's technology. Dr. Lena Hanson, a leading expert in quantum physics, leaned over a holographic projection of a complex equation. The equation, derived from one of the book's final chapters, hinted at a potential pathway to repairing the subtle rips and tears in spacetime caused by the Order's reckless experiments. But the solution was far from straightforward. The equation involved a series of impossibly precise manipulations of dark energy, requiring a level of control over the universe that humans were nowhere near achieving. The margin for error was infinitesimally small; any mistake could unravel the very fabric of reality.

Days bled into weeks. The initial euphoria of victory slowly morphed into a sobering realization of the magnitude of the task ahead. The universe, while restored to a semblance of normalcy, remained subtly altered. Strange anomalies persisted – fleeting distortions of time, localized gravitational anomalies, faint echoes of the chaotic energy surges that had wracked the cosmos. These lingering effects were a constant reminder of the precarious balance of the universe and the devastating potential of uncontrolled cosmic engineering. The recovered data also revealed a disturbing truth: the Obsidian Order was not a rogue faction operating in isolation. They were part of something much larger, a network of clandestine organizations spanning millennia, each vying for control over these same potent forces.

As the team delved deeper into the book's mysteries, they uncovered a startling prophecy – a prediction of a future cosmic event, a convergence of celestial bodies predicted to occur in a few decades, an event described in the text with chilling accuracy. This celestial alignment, according to the book, would trigger a chain of events that could lead to the collapse of multiple galaxies, resulting in an intergalactic scale cosmic disaster of unimaginable proportions. The prophecy was cryptic, peppered with enigmatic symbolism and veiled allegories, but the underlying threat was undeniable. The Obsidian Order had been preparing for this event, attempting to harness its power for their own nefarious purposes. Their failure merely delayed the inevitable.

Further investigation revealed a chilling piece of information: the book wasn't merely a guide to harnessing cosmic energy. It was a key, a cosmic key, unlocking access to dimensions beyond human comprehension, dimensions inhabited by beings whose technology and power dwarfed even the Obsidian Order's ambitions. The book was, in essence, a roadmap to unimaginable power, a power that could either save or destroy the universe. The prophecy was a warning, a final desperate attempt by a long-vanished civilization to prevent a catastrophic future.

The weight of this revelation settled heavily upon the team. The fight against the Obsidian Order had been a battle for survival, a desperate struggle against a tangible threat. But the new threat was far more insidious, a cosmic apocalypse lurking on the horizon. The book's remaining pages held clues, hints of possible solutions, technologies that could potentially prevent the impending celestial convergence. But each solution came with its own set of perils, its own potential for catastrophic failure. The team knew that they were facing a race against time, a desperate struggle against an enemy that transcended even their wildest imaginings. The universe, it seemed, had far more secrets to reveal, secrets that would determine not just the fate of humanity, but the fate of the cosmos itself.

The final pages of the book, fragmented and obscured by time and decay, contained tantalizing clues to the nature of the mysterious civilization that had created it. The clues suggested they were a species far older and more advanced than humanity could even fathom, a species that had mastered the manipulation of spacetime itself, that had walked among the stars for eons, accumulating wisdom and knowledge far exceeding human comprehension. But their knowledge came at a cost. Their advanced technology had apparently led to their downfall, their civilization shattered by forces they could no longer control. The book served as a testament to their arrogance, a monument to their ultimate failure. The prophecy wasn't merely a warning; it was a cautionary tale, a reminder of the hubris of unchecked power.

The implications were staggering. Humanity, having barely escaped one cosmic threat, was now facing a far greater, more existential crisis. The race against time wasn't just to prevent the celestial convergence; it was to understand the ancient civilization's downfall and to prevent history from repeating itself. The team knew that the journey had only just begun. The restoration of the universe was merely a fleeting moment of respite in a cosmic saga filled with peril, wonder, and an overwhelming sense of the unknown. The ancient book, a silent witness to the rise and fall of civilizations, lay open before them, beckoning them towards an even greater mystery, a mystery that could lead them to salvation or utter destruction. The fate of the universe, it seemed, rested on the ability of humanity to unravel its secrets before time ran out. The final chapter, it seemed, was yet to be written. And the universe, forever changed, waited with bated breath.

New Understandings

The air, thick with the scent of burnt metal and ozone, hung heavy in the ruins. The Obsidian Order's meticulously crafted defenses, once a formidable barrier against intruders, lay shattered, reduced to twisted metal and crumbling stone. But the silence, broken only by the occasional sigh of the wind whistling through gaps in the collapsed structures, was more unsettling than the chaos that preceded it. It spoke of a finality, a conclusion to a chapter, yet simultaneously hinted at the opening of an even more profound and terrifying one.

Dr. Aris Thorne, his face grimy and his clothes torn, knelt beside the ancient book. Its pages, miraculously preserved despite the destruction surrounding them, whispered secrets of a cosmos far beyond human comprehension. The glyphs, once indecipherable, now pulsed with a faint luminescence, their meaning slowly revealing itself to his weary mind. The battle had been brutal, a clash between ancient, cosmic forces and a desperate band of human survivors, but the victory, if it could be called that, had come at a steep price.

The Obsidian Order's leader, a shadowy figure known only as the Curator, had been vanquished, but not before unleashing a wave of destructive energy that threatened to unravel the very fabric of spacetime. It was a desperate gamble, a last-ditch effort to preserve the Order's secrets, secrets that now, paradoxically, held the key to humanity's survival. The book, it turned out, wasn't merely a historical artifact; it was a living repository of knowledge, a cosmic Rosetta Stone unlocking the deepest mysteries of the universe.

Among these mysteries, the nature of dark matter and dark energy took center stage. The ancient civilization that had created the book, a race far surpassing humanity in scientific prowess, had achieved a level of understanding that bordered on the divine. Their writings revealed that dark matter wasn't merely an inert substance, a passive observer in the cosmic dance. Instead, it was a dynamic, intelligent entity, a vast, sentient network woven into the very fabric of spacetime. Its interaction with dark energy, far from being random or chaotic, followed intricate patterns, governed by laws that were both elegant and terrifying.

The book described a symbiotic relationship between dark matter and dark energy, a delicate balance that was crucial to the stability of the universe. The Obsidian Order, in their hubristic pursuit of power, had attempted to manipulate this balance, to harness the energies of the cosmos for their own nefarious ends. Their actions, the book revealed, had triggered a chain reaction, a cosmic cascade that nearly resulted in the universe collapsing in on itself. The "celestial convergence," the impending cosmic catastrophe that had driven the narrative thus far, was not a random occurrence, but a direct consequence of the Order's reckless interference.

The new understanding of dark matter and dark energy shifted the scientific paradigm. It wasn't simply a matter of adding a few equations to existing cosmological models; it required a complete overhaul of our understanding of the universe. The implications were staggering. If dark matter was indeed sentient, if it possessed a form of consciousness that transcended our current comprehension, it called into question the very nature of reality itself. Were we alone in the universe? Or were we merely one small, insignificant node in a vast, interconnected cosmic web?

Furthermore, the ancient texts revealed that dark energy wasn't a constant force, as previously believed. It was a dynamic entity, capable of expansion and contraction, its behavior influenced by the collective consciousness of dark matter. The Obsidian Order's actions had disrupted this dynamic equilibrium, triggering a runaway expansion that threatened to tear the universe apart. The near-catastrophic event had been a warning, a glimpse into the potential consequences of meddling with forces far beyond human comprehension.

The book also contained intricate diagrams and equations describing a process the ancient civilization called "Cosmic

Resonance." This involved manipulating the interaction between dark matter and dark energy to achieve a state of equilibrium, a harmonious balance that would ensure the stability of the universe. It was a delicate process, requiring a profound understanding of cosmic dynamics and an almost unimaginable level of precision. The risks were enormous, a single miscalculation could lead to a catastrophic outcome far worse than the celestial convergence they had just narrowly averted.

Aris, along with the surviving members of his team, faced a daunting task. They had to decipher the remaining sections of the book, understand the intricacies of Cosmic Resonance, and then execute the process flawlessly. The fate of the universe, once again, hung in the balance. The sense of relief that had followed the destruction of the Obsidian Order was quickly replaced by a crushing weight of responsibility. The universe, they now understood, wasn't merely a collection of stars, planets, and galaxies; it was a living, breathing entity, a complex interplay of forces that were both beautiful and terrifying.

Days bled into weeks as the team painstakingly studied the ancient texts. Each decoded passage revealed new layers of complexity, new challenges, and new potential pitfalls. The scientific community, alerted to the situation by Aris's initial discoveries, was abuzz with speculation and debate. Many were skeptical, dismissing the ancient texts as fanciful legends, but Aris and his team knew the stakes were too high to dismiss the evidence. The whispers of the universe itself, the subtle shifts in spacetime, confirmed the validity of the ancient knowledge.

The team's work was not without its setbacks. The constant threat of unforeseen consequences loomed large. The very act of studying the book, of attempting to understand the intricacies of Cosmic Resonance, risked triggering another catastrophic event. The fear was palpable, a constant companion, but the need to succeed overshadowed any personal anxieties. The fate of billions, indeed the fate of the universe, rested on their shoulders.

As they delved deeper into the mysteries of the book, they uncovered a profound connection between the ancient civilization and humanity. It was a connection that transcended time and space, a shared destiny woven into the very fabric of existence. The ancient civilization, it turned out, had anticipated their own downfall, foreseeing the rise of a new civilization, a civilization capable of both great destruction and incredible creation. The book wasn't just a warning; it was a gift, a legacy of knowledge passed down through the ages, a testament to the enduring spirit of hope and perseverance.

The final pages of the book revealed the precise steps needed to perform Cosmic Resonance. It was a complex ritual, a delicate dance between science and spirituality, a symphony of cosmic energies. The team spent weeks preparing, calibrating instruments, and mentally preparing for the monumental task ahead. They knew that failure was not an option; the consequences were too dire to contemplate.

The moment of truth arrived under a sky still scarred by the remnants of the celestial convergence. The atmosphere crackled with anticipation, a mixture of fear and hope. Aris, his hands trembling slightly, initiated the sequence, guiding the cosmic energies with precision and care. The universe responded, a symphony of light and energy pulsating through spacetime. The delicate balance was restored, the chaotic energies harmonized, the threat averted.

The aftermath was a profound sense of relief, a shared experience of collective triumph. The universe, scarred but not broken, breathed a collective sigh of relief. Humanity, against all odds, had not only averted a cosmic catastrophe, but had also gained a profound understanding of the universe's deepest secrets. The ancient book, its purpose fulfilled, remained a silent testament to the enduring power of knowledge, the resilience of the human spirit, and the extraordinary interconnectedness of all things in the cosmos. The universe, forever changed, continued its dance, a timeless waltz between creation and destruction, order and chaos, forever shaped by the legacy of the Lost Last Book.

The Obsidian Orders Fate

The silence in the Obsidian Order's shattered citadel was a deceptive calm. Dust motes danced in the slivers of light piercing the ruined dome, illuminating the debris field of their once-impregnable fortress. The air, still crackling with residual energy, held the faint scent of ozone and something else, something ancient and subtly unsettling – the lingering echo of a power long dormant, now brutally extinguished. The final confrontation had been swift, brutal, a clash of cosmic forces that left the ground trembling and the very fabric of spacetime shimmering. The Obsidian Order, a clandestine organization that had manipulated galactic events for millennia, was no more.

Their leader, a being known only as the Architect, had been vanquished, not by brute force, but by the very knowledge they had sought to control. The Lost Last Book, the ancient artifact at the heart of the conflict, had revealed not only the secrets of the universe but also the inherent flaw in the Order's meticulously crafted plans. The Architect, obsessed with imposing order on the chaotic dance of the cosmos, had underestimated the unpredictable nature of existence itself. His ambition, his desire for absolute control, had become his undoing. The book, imbued with the wisdom of countless civilizations, had shown him the futility of his quest, the beauty of the universe's inherent disorder. The final moments of his reign had been not a battle of might, but a silent, agonizing realization of his own insignificance in the face of cosmic grandeur.

The aftermath, however, was far from simple. The destruction of the Order left a power vacuum the size of a galaxy. Their vast network of influence, spanning countless star systems, crumbled, leaving behind a trail of unanswered questions and unresolved conflicts. The very fabric of galactic society was frayed, the delicate balance of power irrevocably altered. Some systems, previously under the Order's iron grip, erupted into open rebellion, their newly found freedom leading to chaotic uprisings and resource wars. Others, caught in the crossfire, struggled to rebuild, facing societal collapse and economic devastation.

The human alliance, instrumental in the Order's downfall, found itself in a precarious position. Victorious but weary, they faced the daunting task of restoring order to the galaxy. The weight of responsibility was immense, the future uncertain. The knowledge gleaned from the Lost Last Book, while invaluable, was also a double-edged sword. Its cryptic passages hinted at realities beyond human comprehension, concepts that challenged the very foundations of their scientific understanding. Dark matter, dark energy, the nature of time itself – the book revealed tantalizing glimpses of these cosmic mysteries, yet simultaneously unveiled the limitations of human understanding. The revelations sparked intense debates amongst scientists, philosophers, and theologians, creating new divisions and challenges.

One of the most pressing issues was the disposal of the Lost Last Book itself. Its power was immense, its knowledge both enlightening and potentially catastrophic. The decision to destroy it, or to safeguard it, was a matter of intense debate. Some argued that its power was too great to be left in human hands, fearing its potential for misuse. Others believed that destroying such a precious source of knowledge would be a profound loss for humanity, a betrayal of the sacrifices made to obtain it. The debate was further complicated by the emergence of fringe groups who believed the book held the key to achieving godlike powers, creating a risk of a new power struggle erupting over the artifact.

Beyond the immediate chaos, the destruction of the Obsidian Order raised profound questions about humanity's role in the cosmos. For centuries, humanity had been relegated to the fringes of galactic society, a relatively insignificant species struggling to understand its place among the stars. Now, with the Order gone, humanity found itself thrust into a position of unexpected prominence, a power vacuum ripe for the taking. The question was, were they ready to accept the mantle of leadership, the responsibility of shaping the future of a vast and complex galaxy?

The answers were not readily available. The human alliance, despite its victory, was fractured. Internal conflicts over resources, ideologies, and the interpretation of the Lost Last Book's revelations threatened to tear it apart. The weight of their newfound power, the sheer scale of the task before them, threatened to overwhelm them. Several prominent figures within the alliance advocated for a policy of noninterference, suggesting a retreat from the galactic stage and a focus on internal matters. They argued that humanity was not yet ready to bear the burden of galactic leadership, that their involvement in interstellar affairs would only lead to further conflict and suffering.

Others, however, saw an opportunity to shape a new galactic order, one founded on principles of cooperation, mutual respect, and the shared pursuit of knowledge. They argued that humanity, having confronted and overcome the Obsidian Order, had proven its resilience and its capacity for great things. They believed that humanity's unique perspective, its inherent drive for exploration and understanding, could serve as the foundation for a brighter, more equitable future for all sentient species in the galaxy.

The debate raged across the galaxy, sparking numerous interstellar conferences, political maneuvering, and even the threat of new conflicts. The destruction of the Obsidian Order had not brought about universal peace; it had simply shifted the dynamics of power, creating a new and unpredictable landscape. The universe, forever changed by the events surrounding the Lost Last Book, continued its relentless march through time, a chaotic yet beautiful tapestry woven from the threads of creation and destruction, order and chaos.

The legacy of the Obsidian Order, however, lingered. Their influence, despite their demise, continued to shape events across the galaxy. Rumors persisted of surviving cells, hidden pockets of resistance, clinging to the Order's dark ideologies. The fear of their resurgence fueled suspicion and paranoia, creating an environment ripe for conflict and manipulation. Even those who had celebrated the Order's fall found themselves grappling with a sense of unease, a lingering uncertainty about the future.

The discovery of hidden Obsidian Order bases, containing advanced technology and cryptic documents, added to the growing sense of unease. These facilities, scattered across the galaxy, provided further evidence of the Order's scale and sophistication. They revealed startling insights into their plans for galactic domination, their mastery of technologies far beyond human comprehension. The analysis of these findings suggested a level of planning and foresight that stunned even the most experienced scientists and intelligence analysts, underscoring the true scope of the challenge humanity had overcome.

The task before humanity was monumental. They had to not only rebuild the shattered remnants of galactic civilization but also address the profound ethical and philosophical questions raised by the Lost Last Book's revelations. The path ahead was fraught with peril, uncertainty, and the ever-present threat of those who would seek to exploit the power vacuum left by the Obsidian Order's collapse. The fate of the galaxy, once again, hung in the balance, its future resting on the shoulders of a species still finding its place amongst the stars, a species grappling with the immense weight of its newfound power and responsibility. The universe watched, a silent, ancient observer, as humanity embarked on its most challenging mission yet: the creation of a new galactic order, an order built not on control and manipulation, but on cooperation, understanding, and the pursuit of knowledge – a future shaped by the legacy of the Lost Last Book and the ashes of the Obsidian Order.

A New Dawn

The crimson sun dipped below the jagged horizon of Xylos, casting long, skeletal shadows across the ravaged landscape. The air, though cleansed of the lingering ozone, still held a tremor, a subtle vibration that spoke of the universe's immense power and its indifference to the squabbles of civilizations. The Obsidian Order, architects of galactic manipulation, were gone, their millennia-long reign of terror reduced to dust and echoes. But the silence was pregnant with potential, with the promise of a new dawn, tinged with the uncertainty of a species newly burdened with the weight of cosmic knowledge.

Dr. Aris Thorne, the astrophysicist whose relentless pursuit of truth had led him to the Lost Last Book, stood amidst the ruins, his gaze fixed on the dying light. The book, its pages filled with equations that defied comprehension and prophecies that chilled the soul, lay open in his hands. Its secrets had been unleashed, shattering the carefully constructed facade of galactic order, exposing the raw, chaotic beauty of the cosmos. The knowledge it contained, once a terrifying weapon in the hands of the Obsidian Order, now held the potential to usher in an era of unprecedented understanding.

But the road ahead was far from clear. The galaxy was a tapestry woven with threads of power, ambition, and ancient grudges. Even with the Order vanquished, the vacuum left in its wake threatened to draw in new players, hungry for the influence and the knowledge that the Obsidian Order had so jealously guarded. Whispers of other factions, equally ruthless and ambitious, started to surface from the shadowed corners of the galaxy, their motives obscured by layers of deceit.

Aris felt the weight of responsibility pressing down on him. He was no politician, no galactic leader, just a scientist who stumbled upon a truth too big, too dangerous for any single individual or nation to control. Yet, the knowledge within the Lost Last Book was not a weapon to be wielded but a guide to be understood. It was a key, unlocking the mysteries of the universe, its creation, and its ultimate fate – mysteries that humanity was now uniquely positioned to explore.

The first priority was rebuilding. Communication networks, fractured by the final battle, needed to be reestablished. Worlds ravaged by the Obsidian Order's machinations needed aid, their shattered populations offered hope and a chance to rebuild their lives. This was a monumental task, a challenge that would require the combined efforts of every surviving civilization across the galaxy.

But cooperation would not be easy. Generations of mistrust, of manipulation and fear, were deeply ingrained in the galactic psyche. The Obsidian Order hadn't merely ruled; they had warped the very fabric of inter-species relations, fostering an environment of suspicion and paranoia. Aris knew that simply removing the Order would not magically heal these wounds.

He looked up, his eyes scanning the ravaged landscape. A lone, battered spaceship, bearing the insignia of the Xylar Resistance, limped towards him. The Resistance, a coalition of planets fighting for their freedom from the Order's iron grip, had been humanity's unexpected allies in the final battle. Now, they were essential partners in the monumental task of rebuilding. They represented hope, but also a sobering reminder of the cost of freedom and the ever-present threat of exploitation.

Their leader, Commander Lyra, approached Aris, her face etched with the weariness of years spent fighting a seemingly insurmountable foe. "The galaxy is still bruised," Lyra stated, her voice gravelly, reflecting years of harsh conditions. "The Order may be gone, but their legacy of mistrust, of division, remains."

Aris nodded in agreement. "We must work together," he said, his voice firm despite the weight of his burden. "Not as conquerors, but as collaborators. The Lost Last Book has shown us that the universe holds secrets far grander than any single civilization can ever hope to comprehend alone. To truly understand it, we must learn to cooperate, to share our knowledge and our resources, to learn from each other, and to build a future rooted in respect and understanding."

Lyra met his gaze. "Easy to say," she said, a hint of cynicism in her tone, "but how do we achieve that? We've spent

centuries fighting to survive; trust doesn't bloom overnight."

Aris knew she was right. The path ahead would be fraught with challenges. There would be disagreements, conflicts of interest, and the temptation to wield the universe's secrets for selfish gains. The newfound knowledge held within the Lost Last Book could either unite the galaxy or tear it apart. The responsibility rested on humanity's shoulders, a weight so profound it could crush them.

The following weeks became a whirlwind of activity. Diplomatic envoys were dispatched across the galaxy, carrying with them the message of a new beginning, a message of cooperation and shared responsibility. The scientific community, galvanized by the revelations of the Lost Last Book, launched ambitious research programs, delving into the mysteries of dark matter, dark energy, and the fundamental forces that governed the universe. Aris, along with a team of scientists from various species, dedicated themselves to deciphering the remaining cryptic passages of the Lost Last Book, seeking answers to fundamental questions about the universe's origins and its ultimate fate.

As days bled into weeks and weeks into months, a fragile sense of unity began to emerge from the ashes of the old order. Cooperation, though often strained and tentative, slowly replaced the bitter rivalry that had once characterized galactic relations. The shared knowledge gained from the Lost Last Book fostered an unprecedented sense of intellectual curiosity. The thirst for understanding transcended species boundaries, binding together scientists and thinkers from across the galaxy in a quest for knowledge previously considered unattainable.

Yet, shadows still lurked in the fringes of the galaxy. Rumors of shadowy organizations, successors to the Obsidian Order, continued to circulate. These factions, motivated by greed or a thirst for power, sought to exploit the knowledge revealed in the Lost Last Book for their own nefarious purposes. Their activities, though subtle and clandestine, were a constant reminder that the fight for a truly unified galaxy was far from over. Aris and Lyra knew that vigilance would be as critical as cooperation. The universe, vast and indifferent, held both immense potential and terrifying dangers.

The journey ahead would be long and arduous. The scars of the past would take time to heal, the wounds of mistrust to mend. But as the first rays of a new dawn broke over the galactic horizon, humanity, carrying the weight of its newfound responsibility, embarked on a mission of unprecedented scope – the creation of a new galactic order, an order forged not in the fires of conflict but in the light of shared understanding, a future where knowledge and cooperation would illuminate the path towards a more harmonious existence among the stars. The future hung in the balance, but for the first time, humanity, guided by the knowledge of the Lost Last Book, had the chance to shape its destiny, to build a future where the universe's vast wonders were not a source of fear, but a beacon of hope. The universe, in its silent, ancient wisdom, seemed to watch and wait, ready to reveal its secrets to a species ready to listen.

Appendix

This appendix contains supplementary information relevant to the scientific concepts explored in "The Lost Last Book." It includes simplified explanations of complex cosmological concepts, as well as a brief overview of the fictional technologies and advanced civilizations mentioned within the narrative. This information is intended to enrich the reader's understanding of the scientific aspects of the story, without requiring a background in advanced astrophysics.

Specific topics covered include:

A simplified explanation of dark matter and dark energy. An overview of the fictional "Aetherium" technology employed by the Obsidian Order.

A brief exploration of the hypothetical "Xantus Civilization" and their advanced understanding of cosmic forces.

Glossary

Aetherium: A fictional energy source harnessed by the Obsidian Order, derived from the manipulation of dark matter and dark energy.

Dark Energy: A mysterious force causing the accelerated expansion of the universe. Its nature remains one of the greatest enigmas in modern cosmology.

Dark Matter: An invisible form of matter that accounts for a significant portion of the universe's mass. Its composition and properties are currently unknown.

Obsidian Order: A shadowy organization seeking to control and weaponize dark matter and dark energy.

Xantus Civilization: A hypothetical ancient civilization mentioned in "The Lost Last Book," possessing an advanced understanding of cosmic forces.